How To Build a New Iraq after Saddam

Patrick Clawson, Editor

THE WASHINGTON INSTITUTE FOR NEAR EAST POLICY

© 2002 by The Washington Institute for Near East Policy

Published in 2002 in the United States of America by The Washington Institute for Near East Policy, 1828 L Street NW, Suite 1050, Washington, DC 20036.

Library of Congress Cataloging-in-Publication Data

How to build a new Iraq after Saddam / Patrick Clawson, editor.
    p. cm.
    Includes bibliographical references.
    ISBN 0-944029-82-5
  1. United States—Politics and government—2001– 2. Iraq—Politics and government—1991– 3. Hussein, Saddam, 1937–
I. Clawson, Patrick, 1951– II. Washington Institute for Near East Policy.
    E902.H69 2002
    327.730567—dc21   2002015563

Cover photo © AP Wide World Photos.
Cover design by Alicia Gansz.

Contributors

Amatzia Baram is director of the Jewish-Arab Center and the Gustav Heinemann Institute for Middle Eastern Studies at the University of Haifa. He is the author of *Building toward Crisis: Saddam Husayn's Strategy for Survival* (The Washington Institute, 1998).

Patrick Clawson is deputy director of The Washington Institute and editor of *Iraq Strategy Review: Options for U.S. Policy* (The Washington Institute, 1998). He is a frequent writer and commentator on U.S. Iraq policy.

Rend Rahim Francke, an Iraqi American, has served as executive director of the Iraq Foundation since 1991. She is a frequent writer on Iraqi politics and is coauthor of *The Arab Shi'a: The Forgotten Muslims* (St. Martin's Press, 2000).

Kamran Karadaghi is deputy director and chief editor of Radio Free Iraq, based in Prague. Formerly a diplomatic and senior political correspondent with *al-Hayat,* he was a 1993 visiting fellow at The Washington Institute.

Ellen Laipson is president and CEO of the Henry L. Stimson Center in Washington, D.C. She previously worked on Middle East issues for the U.S. government, most recently as vice chairman of the National Intelligence Council.

Michael Rubin is a visiting scholar at the American Enterprise Institute. A frequent commentator in electronic and print media, he has traveled widely in Iraq, Iran, Afghanistan, and Sudan.

Safwat Rashid Sidqi is a lawyer and cofounding member of the Kurdistan Human Rights Organization, based in Sulaymaniyah, Kurdistan Region, Iraq.

• • •

Table of Contents

Introduction: Shaping a Stable and Friendly
Post-Saddam Iraq
Patrick Clawson   1

Assessing the Long-Term Challenges
Ellen Laipson   9

The Shape of a New Government
Rend Rahim Francke   19

Minimizing Ethnic Tensions
Kamran Karadaghi   31

Federalism and the Future of Iraq
Michael Rubin   44

A Criminal Regime: Accountability in a
Post-Saddam Iraq
Safwat Rashid Sidqi   56

Viewing Regime Change through a Historical Lens
Amatzia Baram   69

Maps
  Iraq: No-Fly Zones and Kurdish Areas   vi
  Iraq: Provinces and Capitals   vii

Iraq: No-Fly Zones and Kurdish Areas

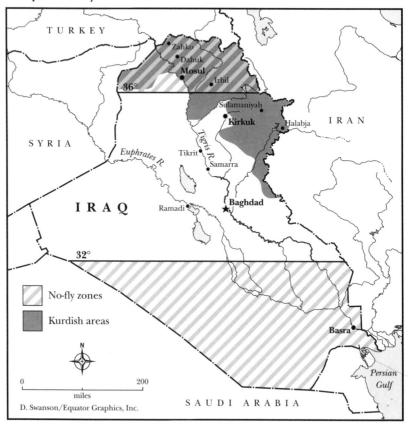

TURKEY

Zahko
Dahuk
Mosul
Irbil
36°

Sulamaniyah
Kirkuk
Halabja

IRAN

SYRIA

Euphrates R.
Tikrit
Samarra

Tigris R.

IRAQ

Ramadi
★ **Baghdad**

32°

No-fly zones

Kurdish areas

N

0   200
miles

D. Swanson/Equator Graphics, Inc.

SAUDI ARABIA

Basra

Persian Gulf

Iraq: Provinces and Capitals

Patrick Clawson

Introduction: Shaping a Stable and Friendly Post-Saddam Iraq

Whether changing the regime in Baghdad is a worthwhile U.S. policy depends in no small part on defining the shape that Iraq would most likely assume following Saddam Husayn's removal. Among other central objectives, any strategy for regime change should include the long-term goal of creating a stable and friendly Iraq. Toward this end, the five essays in this monograph explore the most urgent challenges that a post-Saddam Iraq would likely present. Although this study is not predicated on any one assumption about the possible mechanisms of regime change, the authors do address many of the special problems that would arise if Saddam were removed by means of a U.S. invasion. They also discuss measures that could be taken to reduce potential future threats from Iraq.

Territorial Integrity

Despite their many serious concerns about how Iraq will fare after Saddam, the authors seem to agree that preserving Iraq's territorial integrity should not pose a major challenge. This view flies in the face of a frequently heard argument in the West, where many analysts warn of the serious danger that a post-Saddam Iraq could split into three parts along ethnic lines: Kurdish, Shi'i Arab, and Sunni Arab.[1]

One reason why Iraq is likely to remain intact is that it is entirely dependent on oil income. Control of Iraq's oil income means control of Iraq itself; it is a powerful glue holding the country together. This factor would become all the more

1

important if Iraq were able to increase oil production to at least six million barrels per day within the first decade after Saddam's removal; even at the modest price of $15 per barrel, this production level would generate nearly $33 billion in annual revenue. None of the three major Iraqi ethnic groups would be willing to forego a share of such revenue by seceding.

For example, the most obvious candidates for independence are the Kurds. Yet, even those who call for an independent Kurdistan insist that any such entity be granted control over the oil fields near the present Kurdish autonomous region in northern Iraq—a scenario that the rest of the country would never accept.

Moreover, if non-Kurdish Iraqis were too weak and divided to prevent a Kurdish bid for independence, the Kurds would still face the insurmountable opposition of Turkey. The broad consensus among the Turkish public and elite is that an independent Kurdistan carved from northern Iraq would destabilize Kurdish-majority southeastern Turkey, rekindling the violence in which 30,000 Turks and Kurds died during the 1990s. Even in the unlikely event that Iran and Syria acquiesced to the independence of Iraqi Kurdistan, Turkey would almost certainly use military force to prevent the breakup of Iraq, with strong political support from the Arab world.

Given these factors, Iraq's territorial integrity would probably remain unaffected in the wake of Saddam's removal. In fact, Iraq's heavy dependence on oil suggests that the country would continue its modern tradition of strong central governments, much like other oil-dependent countries worldwide. Unfortunately, oil-rich states are typically run by authoritarians who use oil income to preserve their undemocratic rule; modern Iraq is no exception, having seen one strongman after another ignore representative institutions. Moreover, the central role of oil does not necessarily bode well for political stability; immense oil riches are such a tempting prize that various groups may contest for control over the state.

Maintaining Stability

In fact, political instability is a much more substantial threat than the division of Iraq into ethnic ministates. Most worrisome is the prospect of revolving-door governments; after all, Iraq experienced a succession of bloody coups from 1958 until Saddam consolidated power in the late 1970s. After his removal, the cycle of coups could resume for a number of reasons (e.g., the strong tribal influences among the army officer corps or the highly competitive relationship between the major tribes). In the worst-case scenario, Iraq could perhaps come to resemble 1960s-era Syria, where coups were so frequent that the government ceased to function effectively, while foreign forces meddled by backing different groups of officers. That would be a tragedy for the Iraqi people and a source of instability for the entire region, not least because Iraq would become ripe ground for radical movements promising to resurrect the country's greatness.

Revolving-door Iraqi governments would pose a host of problems for U.S. policymakers as well. These problems could prove even more challenging than those that would arise if the United States were to occupy Iraq in the style of post–World War II Germany and Japan. Planning for potential occupation does not necessarily cover the worst-case scenario that could emerge following regime change. In fact, the problems posed by successive coups would be vastly different from those posed by a lengthy Allied-style occupation and, in their own ways, just as complicated.

For example, an initial coup could occur during the course of U.S. military operations. That is, once U.S. forces degraded the Iraqi Republican Guard (RG) and Special Republican Guard (SRG), commanders in the regular army could seize the opportunity to topple Saddam before the United States destroyed them as well. Such a circumstance would put Washington in a difficult position. For instance, these commanders could prove unwilling to surrender Iraq's weapons of mass destruction (WMD), which so many in the Iraqi military see as the principal means by which their country was saved from conquest by Iran during the 1980s. Alternately, a group of generals could announce that they were taking charge at a time when Saddam's whereabouts were unknown and when significant military forces were still fighting on his behalf; in this case, the United States would have to decide whether or not to provide military support to potentially unfamiliar new leaders.

Even if a new regime were established after, rather than during, a U.S. military campaign, the first government to replace Saddam could falter quickly if U.S. forces did not intervene to prevent coups. Faced with vaguely similar situations in Korea and South Vietnam in the 1960s, the United States chose an unsuccessful policy of standing aside during coup attempts. If such a policy were adopted in Iraq, a coup could produce a successor regime that renounces commitments made by an initial, more favorable post-Saddam government (e.g., to give up WMD). For this reason, even if the first new regime were imperfect, the U.S. military would face strong pressure to protect it from coups.

In such a case, however, the United States would in effect become responsible for how well the new Iraqi government functioned, since American forces would be propping it up. Moreover, given the currently widespread support for democratization, Washington would likely be called on to push Baghdad toward more representative governance. Such an assignment could enlarge exponentially, with the United States eventually attempting to remake Iraqi society into a fully functioning Western-style democracy, as it did during its postwar occupation of Japan.

Short of full occupation, however, U.S. forces would be constrained by the need to respect the sovereignty and authority of a new, imperfect Iraqi government. This constraint would complicate the already difficult task of remaking Iraq, magnifying the potential for nationalist resentment against the U.S. presence. A full occupation would be bad enough in the eyes of the most ardent Iraqi nationalists; an Iraqi government nominally in charge but in practice dependent on U.S. support could fare even worse, particularly if it faced constant U.S. pressure to remake the country along American lines. In short, occupying Iraq would be a challenge, but preserving Iraqi stability and friendship without occupation could prove even more difficult, unless some way were found to minimize the threat of successive post-Saddam coups.

The Iraqi Military

Just as territorial integrity is not the principal problem that a post-Saddam Iraq would face, so the country's ethnic groups are not necessarily the key social actors to watch. If the risk of successive coups is paramount, then the key actor is the Iraqi army.

Focusing on the role of the army in a post-Saddam Iraq may at first seem unwarranted; after all, Saddam would most likely be toppled by overwhelming U.S.-led military action, which would in turn destroy much of Iraq's own military. Yet, military planners should distinguish between the RG/SRG and the regular Iraqi army when outlining potential campaigns against Saddam. Given their history, the RG and SRG would likely proffer intense resistance in order to preserve Saddam's rule. For example, they continued to fight resolutely in 1991 even after it became readily apparent that Iraq was destined for a crushing defeat at the hands of the U.S.-led coalition. Moreover, soldiers in these units appear to have been carefully selected and trained to ensure their loyalty to Saddam. They have benefited personally from his rule and would have reason to fear bloody reprisals against them in the wake of his removal.

The regular Iraqi army is a different story altogether. Although the United States has ample cause to destroy the RG and SRG, U.S. military leaders may want to spare Iraq's regular army, if for no other reason than the fact that it is a much less potent military opponent than the RG and SRG. In fact, the regular army could decide to stay on the sidelines of a conflict with U.S.-led forces, and many of its soldiers could in turn desert. The United States might even be able to persuade Iraqi brigade or division commanders to defect, especially if Iraqi opposition elements and U.S. Special Forces operatives could assure them that they would be protected from the retaliation of units loyal to Saddam. Although defecting units may have little to offer in the military sense, they could play other important roles in a post-Saddam Iraq.

In fact, few Iraqi institutions would have more potential value in the immediate aftermath of regime change than the regular army. If Iraqi army units were left intact following a U.S.-led military campaign, they could play a key role in maintaining order. Moreover, because much of the Iraqi public still respects the regular army, generals could become important figures in a new government, even if that government were largely civilian and designed by an internationally sponsored reconciliation summit similar to the 2001 Bonn conference on post-Taliban Afghanistan. As a well-regarded, functioning institution in a country whose civil society has been decimated by Saddam's totalitarian regime, the regular army would have much to offer a new government.

Yet, the army could just as well become a den of coup-plotters, with officers from each major tribe seeking control of a post-Saddam central government. Those shaping a post-Saddam Iraq would therefore face a difficult task: taking advantage of the army's assets while forestalling power bids by its officers. The authors in this study offer several different ideas for solving that problem. Good arguments could be made for placing the regular army under strong civilian leadership, yet there are equally cogent arguments for assigning the army a prominent role in a new government. In any case, this is an especially important issue that requires careful consideration.

The Advantages of Liberation

Although achieving battlefield success against the Iraqi military would not be easy, ensuring a stable and friendly post-Saddam Iraq would pose even greater challenges. Therefore, this more difficult task should guide the formation of military strategy. A strategy that ensured victory over the Iraqi military would be of little value if it prevented the United States and its allies from achieving their larger goal—stability and responsible leadership for Iraq. Military planners should therefore devote special attention to the potential influence that their operations could have on a post-Saddam Iraq.

As discussed in the previous section, a strategy that targeted the RG and SRG while bypassing the regular army could prove to be of enormous value, despite its risks. An even more ambitious strategy, however, would be to give Iraqis themselves as much credit as possible for the defeat of Saddam's forces, allowing them to feel greatly responsible for his overthrow—in other words, a strategy of liberation rather than occupation. The more pride that Iraqis felt about removing Saddam, the more likely they would be to identify with the government that replaced him. Such a government would have much stronger nationalist credentials than a government imposed by outsiders. For example, consider the role played by French Resistance forces during the Nazi occupation of their country. Although they had little military impact on the eventual liberation of France, their postwar sociopolitical impact was considerable.

A liberation strategy would in part be a matter of presentation, that is, of assigning credit to whatever Iraqi forces participated in the fight against Saddam, even if their role were actually marginal. Such a strategy suggests that the U.S. military role on the ground should be kept as small and discreet as possible, with significant attention devoted to encouraging the defection of Iraqi army units. Those who argue for minimizing the participation of U.S. ground forces have been accused of favoring a cut-rate approach to regime change, as opposed to committing a larger force that would presumably guarantee success. Some adherents of this minimalist strategy may in fact be motivated by cost considerations. Others, however, seem to be concentrating on winning the larger war rather than simply achieving battlefield success. In their view, victory entails the Iraqi people taking significant credit for liberating their country, which would in turn maximize the chances that they would embrace their post-Saddam government.

Whatever the weaknesses of a liberation strategy, it has one vital strength: it concentrates on the most difficult problem of all, that of putting Iraqi society back together after Saddam. Any strategy for regime change should begin with an explanation of how it would deal with this greater challenge and, from there, discuss the best means of replacing the present regime.

Note

1. The split between Shi'i and Sunni Arabs is about social background, not religious beliefs, so it is more appropriate to view it as an ethnic rather than a religious division; an example of the latter is the division between moderate Muslims and radical Islamists.

Ellen Laipson
Assessing the Long-Term Challenges

As Washington debates policies for regime change in Iraq, the question of when change occurs may ultimately prove more important than how it occurs. Military strategists and planners are focusing on invasion scenarios, and pundits are weighing whether the Bush administration has already moved beyond coup plotting and opposition-led options. But the real story of what becomes of Iraq after Saddam Husayn may be determined more by how long he remains in power than by the details of his demise.

The following analysis of transition in Iraq is predicated on three assumptions:

1. The only practical definition of a "post-Saddam" regime is one in which neither Saddam nor his immediate Tikriti entourage is in power. Aside from that criterion, anything is possible: chaos, military government, Ba'ath rule, multiparty coalitions, Shi'i dominance, de facto division of the country into two or three parts, et cetera.

2. Although the immediate successor to Saddam may be a marginal, transitional figure or group, any planning for a post-Saddam Iraq should take a longer-term view of the country, its society, and its potential for stability.

3. The role of the international community will be less pivotal than expected. First, its influence may well be diffused among competing players with different agendas. Second, the durability of change will be determined by Iraqis themselves through their capacity for rebuilding not only the physical aspects of their lives, but the political and social life of the country as well.

9

Timing is crucial; the longer Saddam rules, the more difficult it will be to rebuild a modern, functioning society once he is gone. Many of the prominent exiles who came of age during the good years of Ba'ath rule and became the well-educated elite that built modern Iraq are still in their productive years; nevertheless, they are approaching retirement. Should regime change occur soon, this generation of professionals, still perhaps favorably disposed to the West, would be able to play an important role, if not in leadership positions then in advisory roles. If change does not occur for several years, however, most of the working-age population would likely be composed of people whose entire adult lives have been shaped by the harsh realities of Iraq's decline: namely, the 1980s, with the economic costs of the war against Iran; the 1990s, with international sanctions and Saddam's excesses; and the new millennium, which has seen some material relief from sanctions but continued political and social brutality.

Iraq's Potential

Two quite different realities tend to shape an outsider's thinking about post-Saddam Iraq. On the one hand, Iraq has tremendous potential to become a successful state. It has natural resources, a tradition of strong (too strong, perhaps) institutions, and remarkable human resources. In a sense, Saddam's ambitions and investments have placed Iraq in an enviable position compared to other Arab states in terms of education, infrastructure, and societal achievements.[1] The Iraqi elite have enjoyed higher standards of education, greater opportunities for travel and training abroad, and more governmental support in the arts and sciences than most of their Arab confreres.

On the other hand, the many deleterious changes that have occurred in Iraq over the past two decades have undoubtedly had a profound effect on the elite's psyche and political orientation, and the erosion of socioeconomic conditions may warrant more modest forecasts about Iraq's short- to medium-term potential:

- Literacy in the early 1980s was estimated at 80 percent, and primary-school enrollment was free and virtually universal. Although reliable data is scarce two decades later, education has clearly become too costly for many, and literacy rates have dropped. Some estimate that as many as a third of Iraqi children do not attend school, either because schools are not available, because of economic duress, or both.
- Per capita income is probably less than one-quarter of its 1980 level of more than $4,000, and as many as 80 percent of Iraqis live below the poverty line, nearly double the number of a decade ago.[2]
- Health standards in the 1980s were higher than the regional average, although rural poverty and disease were a chronic problem. Currently, international health experts (whose objectivity is sometimes questioned due to overreliance on Iraqi statistics) report that conditions have worsened dramatically for Iraqis. Alarming increases have been noted in infectious disease, infant mortality, and rare cancers. Among the causes of this unfortunate development are the regime's use of chemical weapons and its mismanagement of the United Nations (UN) oil-for-food program.

Iraqi society has been brutalized and traumatized over the past half-century, and such conditions have taken a toll on Iraqi confidence in the future. Outsiders simply cannot know how the minds and political aspirations of Iraqi citizens have been shaped by the many years of Saddam's rule. Ample anecdotal reporting shows that Iraqis universally loathe Saddam[3] and would rejoice at his demise. One can assume that most of the population hopes to return to a time when Iraq was widely respected for its prosperity and feared as a powerful regional force. Presumably, Iraqis would unite around the prospect of positive change and healing that Saddam's departure would portend.

Yet, outsiders should not be surprised if a generation of Iraqis who have lived solely under Saddam's rule reflexively seek strong leadership once he is gone, expecting the state to tell them what to do and to set limits on their freedoms. Many in Iraq speak of their yearning for democracy once change comes, but it would be unfair to expect the citizenry to learn how to become democrats overnight. Like the citizens of the former republics of the Soviet Union, many Iraqis, acculturated as they are to a strongman model, may revert to nondemocratic behavior, particularly if crime and disorder prevail when the Tikritis fall. Many Iraqis living in exile and in liberated northern Iraq are also predisposed to a perhaps excessive degree of respect for authority figures, even while speaking of pluralism and representative government. Such an attitude could undermine the healthy questioning of authority that is the hallmark of most democratic societies.

The effects of brutalization may also manifest themselves in harsh attitudes toward the international community. Iraqis who are currently in their thirties or forties may harbor deep resentment toward the West generally and the United States in particular, even if they are willing to work with Westerners toward the liberation of their country. Owing to the regime's propaganda and to the material conditions of their lives, many Iraqis do not appreciate the nuances of Western sanctions policies, and they may have formed political views that are based on supposed Western ill will toward their country. A post-Saddam government may therefore project deep animus toward the West, placing Iraq in a defiant and fiercely independent posture in its regional and international relations.

Internal Transition Issues

In comparison to the enormous efforts required in Afghanistan, the physical repair of Iraq will be relatively easy. Iraq is a country of engineers and builders, people who quickly restored bridges and roads after the Iran-Iraq and Gulf Wars. Recent visitors to Iraq report both urban and rural disrepair owing to economic constraints, but once regime change occurs, the availability of material and know-how should permit fairly straightforward reconstruction. The disbursement of existing funds for food, medicine, and other civilian purposes should bring about rapid improvement of basic economic conditions, including badly needed repairs of public works (e.g., water systems, hospitals). The potential fate of Saddam's palaces under a successor government could prove interesting: would they be preserved as museums to record the folly and excess of his rule, torn down by angry mobs, or maintained by a new class of selfish brutes? Whatever the case, Iraq need not be a permanent welfare state; it has adequate natural and human resources to meet the challenge of rebuilding.

Far more important will be social and political repair, both of which will pose a daunting challenge. For example, the reintegration of the Kurdish north is not a given; its brighter economic conditions, freer political environment, and indisputable preference for autonomy mean that the Kurds would have few incentives to regard a unified Iraq as more desirable than their recent, impressive self-governing experience. Should a sense of Iraqi patriotism and the international community's inducements convince them to work toward Iraqi unity, the Kurds could rightfully claim an important role in the transition. As major players in the various iterations of the united Iraqi opposition, the Kurds hosted the Iraqi National Congress during the critical years in which it operated on Iraqi soil, before the regime's incursion into Irbil in September 1996. The two Kurdish party leaders, Masud Barzani and Jalal Talebani (heads of the Kurdistan Democratic Party and the Patriotic Union of Kurdistan, respectively), are currently on good terms because they are running their respective zones of northern Iraq separately; both would be legitimate claimants to seats in a collective leadership arrangement for all of Iraq.

Yet, Sunnis from the heartland of Iraq, along with the country's beleaguered Shi'i majority, would almost certainly have other ideas. The Sunnis are disproportionately represented in the leadership of the key national institutions (including the army), and their active participation in a successor government would therefore be vital to national stability. Whether the Shi'is believe that power would shift to them in a more representative system is not clear. Those Shi'is who dare to be politically active in the current system appear to hold a wide range of different political views. Many have been co-opted by the regime and have cast their lot with the incumbent elite, while others have Islamist or leftist leanings. Still others are active in the pluralistic opposition groups and profess to embrace a democratic future for Iraq.

Aside from issues of representation under a new regime, many more immediate problems would affect relations between the Kurds, Sunnis, and Shi'is. Should law and order—already reported to be quite precarious—erode further, vendettas and bloodletting among these groups could erupt and become difficult to suppress. For example, Kurds displaced from regime-controlled towns in the north (e.g., Mosul) by Saddam's Arabization drive may want to reclaim their property. Similarly, many Shi'is, including those in the holy cities of Najaf and Karbala in central Iraq, hold deep grievances over their treatment by mainly Sunni-led security forces, indicating that intercommunal violence could well occur in various parts of the country. Such tensions could become an enduring problem for Iraq, one possibly exacerbated by the emergence of political parties based on communal identity.

The reintegration of even a modest proportion of the estimated four million Iraqi exiles could also have a wide impact on the post-Saddam transition, particularly in terms of revenue flows and the inculcation of ideas of tolerance and political openness acquired abroad. Yet, Iraqis who have endured Saddam's rule may feel a greater entitlement to positions of privilege and leadership, and tensions could well arise between them and newly returned émigrés who had been spared the physical deprivations of life inside Iraq.[4] Exiled Iraqis would no doubt have a difficult time establishing their political bona fides in post-Saddam Iraq, especially if no clearly accepted leader emerged among them. Competition among the returnees can be assumed; consensus on who speaks for them is highly unlikely. Although the potential economic, political, and social pressures of rapid repatriation should not be underestimated, both Iraqis and the international community would likely view the return of émigré Iraqis as a sign of a society making itself whole again.

Regional Impact

Iraq's neighbors—all of whom are experiencing their own problems of governance and economic insufficiencies—will find the transition to the post-Saddam era unsettling. The Western view that change in Iraq would remove a serious security threat from the region is not held by all; some rationalize that a weak, contained Iraq is manageable and perhaps preferable to a newly empowered and accepted Iraq. In the event of regime change, neighboring countries could face immediate challenges from associates of Saddam's regime who, fearing retribution, flee Iraq and seek asylum or safe passage elsewhere. Moreover, concerns about lawlessness in Iraq could lead its neighbors to bolster their border defenses and place their armed forces on alert.

Regional leaders are even more uncertain about the political direction that a post-Saddam Iraq could take, including its potential impact on political forces in their own countries. Some leaders may fear that change in Iraq could unleash demands for similar change at home. Jordan, for one, could weather a post-Saddam transition, particularly if Jordanians were still preoccupied with the Palestinian quagmire. Moreover, Jordan is generally sympathetic with the Iraqi people and would benefit from the revitalization of the Iraqi economy. Similarly, the Gulf states would embrace a post-Saddam Arab leader and would seek assurances that their blood feud with Iraq was over.

In Turkey and Iran, the uncertainties may be greater. Ankara would not sit idly if it perceived that the Kurds were exploiting a power vacuum in Baghdad. For its part, Tehran has grown accustomed to a weak Iraq and would worry about latent hegemonic intentions in the minds of any Iraqi successor regime.

The West, and the United States in particular, would need to watch inter-Arab dynamics carefully in the wake of Saddam's ouster. Common sense dictates that a new leader in Baghdad would attempt to appear nonthreatening and to ingratiate himself with current Western leaders, in addition to seeking rapid normalization of political and trade ties. But other scenarios are possible.

For example, should the Arab-Israeli zone still be in acute agitation when Iraqi regime change occurs, the new leader in Baghdad could serve as a galvanizing force in the Arab world, reestablishing Iraq's leadership credentials by striking out boldly on the Palestinian issue. Although incumbent regimes look to the Arab League summit communiqué and Saudi Crown Prince Abdullah's peace plan as the coordinated Arab position on this issue, a new Iraqi leader could stake out a more defiant position that attracts large segments of Arab society by openly criticizing the more cautious approach of other regimes. This is not to suggest that Iraq would intervene militarily, but it could offer new moral support for Palestinian violence or question the Arab consensus in troublesome ways. By exploiting both the palpable anger seen across the Arab world and the presumably strong anti-American attitudes inside Iraq itself, a new Iraqi regime could assume leadership of a more radical, rejectionist Arab approach to the Palestinian issue, creating momentum that would have a chilling effect on moderate positions.

Iraq and the International Community

Regime change in Baghdad would give the international community a chance to work collectively on healing the wounds of the past decade and transforming Iraq from a source of menace to a source of regional stability. The strong international coalition forged in 1990 to oust Iraq from Kuwait has eroded over such problems as Iraqi noncompliance with UN resolutions on weapons. Tensions have increased recently over U.S. intentions and policies regarding regime change.

Once change occurs, however, those countries with a stake in Iraq's future, including Middle Eastern neighbors, major European trading partners, and Russia, can begin a new chapter. Most everyone in the international community would be eager to help a new regime in Iraq establish itself, manage law and order internally, and begin the process of reconciliation and reconstruction. Aid in support of humanitarian relief, infrastructure improvements, and institution building would likely flow from a plethora of international organizations, foundations, and nongovernmental organizations. The reestablishment of human ties with Iraqi civil society would also be critical. Cultural exchanges and training programs would be particularly important in updating Iraqis on what has been happening in civil society elsewhere in the Arab world and beyond.

At the same time, the international community would demand that the new regime declare its peaceful intentions toward its neighbors and commit itself to meaningful limitations on armaments. The details of these commitments would be enshrined in new UN resolutions or legally binding agreements. Western allies may well differ somewhat over the extent of this disarmament. Whatever the case, a post-Saddam Iraq should be permitted an effective modern military that could fulfill basic defensive requirements and retain its status as an elite institution in the country.

In fact, controlling Iraqi ambition while preserving a healthy sense of national identity and pride will be one of the key challenges once Saddam is removed. After all, the international community's dispute is with Saddam's regime; any strategy that aims to make Iraq a permanently weak state or that appears punitive to Iraqi society would be shortsighted. Policymakers would do well to recall that America's treatment of Japan's emperor as the embodiment of Japanese identity proved to be an inspired piece of statesmanship following World War II. The United States should permit, even encourage, Saddam's successor to express pride in Iraq's history and achievements—to highlight elements of Iraq's pre-Saddam past that will help unite the country and give the Iraqi people hope for the future.

Ultimately, the role that a post-Saddam Iraq plays in the region—whether of regional hegemon or cooperative neighbor—will be determined by a number of factors: Will Iraq's neighbors be confident enough domestically to establish a new regional security dialogue? Will the United States be able to shape that debate? Will the Arab-Israeli conflict become a permanent preoccupation, or will progress be made toward resolution? Will Iran become a reliable regional partner, or will it pose new risks to Iraq that drive the security calculations of a new regime in Baghdad? How the United States comes to view Iraqi power and potential once Saddam is gone will be determined in part by the answers to these questions. U.S. policies will play a critical role in reaching those answers; the rest is up to the Iraqis themselves.

Notes

1. Some question whether Iraq is in fact that far ahead of other Arab societies. See Isam al-Khafaji, "The Myth of Iraqi Exceptionalism," *Middle East Policy* 7, no. 4 (October 2000), pp. 62–86. Looking at socioeconomic indicators in the aggregate, al-Khafaji makes a compelling case that Iraq at its peak was not significantly different from other Arab states. My argument here, however, focuses more on the technocratic elite.

2. See, for example, the "Country Reports" on Iraq offered by Social Watch, a nongovernmental watchdog organization that monitors poverty worldwide (available on the group's website: www.socialwatch.org).

3. See, for example, Mark Bowden's gripping article "Tales of the Tyrant," *Atlantic Monthly* 289, no. 5 (May 2002), p. 53.

4. Similar political dynamics were seen between Palestinians who remained under Israeli occupation and those who lived in exile with Yasir Arafat. In that case, however, the returnees were accorded instant legitimacy by their association with the Palestinian leader.

Rend Rahim Francke

The Shape of a
New Government

M any have argued that the shape of the government that
replaces Saddam Husayn will largely depend on the
manner in which his regime is overthrown. This view repre-
sents lazy thinking, at best, or a shirking of responsibility, at
worst. The mechanism of regime change will not be the only
determining factor in the makeup of a post-Saddam Iraq. A
host of other forces will come into play, including regional
and international expectations and domestic pressures.

What Types of Government Are Possible?

At least three types of successor government are theoretically
possible following U.S.-led military action aimed at overthrow-
ing Saddam's regime:

*A continuity government formed after an eleventh-hour palace
coup by senior officials within Saddam's regime.* This would likely
result in a reformed and expanded Ba'ath leadership dominated by holdover civilians from Tikrit and the surrounding
provinces. Although a continuity government would likely
preserve the structure of the Iraqi state and leave many state
institutions intact, it would nevertheless reform the Revolutionary Command Council (RCC), the Ba'ath Regional
Command, the National Assembly, and the intelligence and
security organs. Such a government would appeal to the con-
servative nature of Arab politics and find favor with regimes
in the Persian Gulf and the Levant.

*A military government emerging from a last-minute military coup
that capitalizes on the impending defeat of the regime by outside forces.*
This would likely dissolve some of the civilian institutions of

19

the state (e.g., the RCC, Ba'ath Regional Command, and National Assembly), as well as the paramilitary groups directly associated with Saddam. Other so-called national military and security organizations (e.g., the Republican Guard and the Iraqi Intelligence Service) would likely be preserved with some modification. The long suit of this government would be law and order; it could appeal to fearful Arab states by promising internal stability.

A national unity government resulting from a strategy of "managed change" that ushers in a one- to two-year transition to constitutional status. This coalition would include a diversity of interests representing the multiple political and social constituencies in Iraq. A national unity government would dismantle the RCC, the Ba'ath Regional Command, the National Assembly, and the paramilitary organizations and seek a deep restructuring of traditional military and security organizations. By doing so, the government would signal more radical structural change than either of the first two options and herald a new direction in Iraqi politics. Yet, it would have far greater difficulty appealing to regional states wary of such revolutionary change.

Immediate Challenges

Whatever the profile and composition of a new government, its greatest challenge would be ensuring peace and stability in its first several years. Stability will require more than simply providing enough troops and police forces; it will also depend on creating a political climate that invites cooperation and mitigates the causes of dissent. A new government would need to secure domestic credibility and cooperation, negotiate political rivalries and challenges, counter foreign meddling and domestic subversion, and preserve Iraq's territorial integrity.

As a subset of these overarching requirements, a new government would have to deal with multiple problems and prove its competence and credibility from the instant it assumed power. First, it would have to fulfill humanitarian needs and vital services, a formidable task requiring the goodwill and assistance of the international community. Second, it would have to preserve law and order at multiple levels, from preventing vigilantism and acts of personal revenge to controlling looting, arson, and other kinds of violence. This would create a dilemma; although effective, well-trained security and police forces would be essential to a new regime's success, the country's existing security organizations are universally hated by Iraqis, in addition to being heavily compromised. Third, a new government would have to gain the confidence of its neighbors and the international community. Post-Saddam Iraq will need the help of regional and Western countries, yet its neighbors will be watching the country's transition warily and may not be prepared to give a new government the benefit of the doubt.

Regional Pressures

Regionally, a successor government would be pressured by the shared fears and competing interests of neighboring countries. All of Iraq's neighbors fear the post-Saddam potential for disorder, intervention by other states, and consequent destabilization of their own domestic affairs. Additionally, despite pious talk about keeping Iraq militarily strong, none of the governments in the region want to foster a militarily resurgent Iraq. On the contrary, they all want a relatively weak Iraq that is considerate of their domestic needs and exigencies.

The countries that would exert the greatest pressure on a post-Saddam Iraq are Saudi Arabia, Turkey, and Iran. The Saudis fear the possibility of Shi'i dominance, democratizing trends, loss of oil revenue, and Baghdad's emergence as Washington's new principal ally in the region. Saudi interests favor a continuation of the status quo insofar as possible, with a Sunni-dominated centralized government (albeit civilian in nature) under international constraints.

Iran fears three potential post-Saddam scenarios: the remilitarization of Iraq; the sanctioning of Kurdish autonomy or federalism; or a return to the 1980s U.S. policy of favoring Baghdad over Tehran and using Iraqi territory as a military or political launchpad against Iran. Tehran would welcome visible Shi'i (preferably Islamist) participation in a new Iraqi government, as well as expansion of trade with Iraq.

The overriding fear in Ankara is of Kurdish autonomy or federalism, which could undermine Turkey's control over its own Kurdish population. To that end, Ankara is strengthening its support for Turkoman demands as a counterbalance to Kurdish demands, with an eye toward the oil-rich regions of Mosul and Kirkuk.

Other neighboring countries such as Syria harbor various combinations of these fears and ambitions. All would watch a new Iraqi government closely for signs of threat or promise.

International Pressures

International pressures would be decisive in shaping the policies of an Iraqi successor government. In addition to expecting stability and moderation in foreign affairs, European countries and the United States would demand compliance with United Nations resolutions, including full access for weapons inspectors. Economic interests would play a major role in defining relations with a successor government, and intense international economic competition in the oil sector would force a new regime to make difficult and sensitive decisions in its efforts to please all and antagonize none.

Moreover, in the wake of a successful intervention, the international community, especially the United States, would gain its greatest leverage over Baghdad since the end of World War II. America and its allies would have power not only over weapons inspections and foreign policy, but also over domestic policies and institutional arrangements. Consequently, regardless of the mechanisms of regime change, the nature of a new government would greatly depend on two factors: 1) how the West viewed the political future of Iraq and the region as a whole, and 2) whether the West was prepared to commit to nation building in Iraq. If the leverage available to the West were used constructively, it would contribute much to the healthy and peaceful revival of Iraq.

Domestic Pressures

The first task of any new government in Iraq would be to ensure internal peace and stability, without which no other challenges could be met. Securing peace would depend on the government's ability to gain the trust and cooperation of the diverse political and social sectors within Iraq. Failing that, the new regime would face unrest, including armed resistance, subversive activities, and attempts at military coups. Such failure would be the chief impetus for external intervention and separatist tendencies, the very dangers that other countries in the region fear most.

In addition, the severity of the current regime's repression has created a cauldron of grievances and anger that has been gathering steam under the surface of Iraqi politics for the past two decades. The combination of the Gulf War and the expansion of democracy around the world has given victimized political and social groups in Iraq aspirations to political recognition and participation following Saddam's removal. The most tangible example of these aspirations can be found among the Kurds, who have significantly developed their local institutions during their ten years of autonomy, however imperfectly. There is no turning back for the Kurds; any new government must heed their interests if Iraq's territorial integrity is to be preserved.

The Kurds are only the most obvious instance of rising expectations among Iraqis. Several Shi'i religious groups are now fighting Saddam's regime in southern Iraq, and many are already demanding full political status and participation in a future government.[1] The Turkomans, long a quiet community, are making similar claims. Even rival Sunni clans, entrenched in the army and security organs, pose competing challenges to Saddam's regime. Moreover, all of these groups are armed to one degree or another. None of them would countenance exclusion from post-Saddam political arrangements; nothing less than a seat at the table or a fight for recognition would satisfy them.

A primary challenge for a new regime would be the need to create common ground among these various constituencies. The pressure placed on the Iraqi population during the past twenty years of war (both internal and external), repression, and international sanctions has led to a fracturing of Iraqi society and a retreat to reductionist loyalties. These divisions are not as simplistic as "Kurds versus Arabs" or "Shi'is versus Sunnis." Today, Iraqi allegiances are far more clan-based and narrowly local. Within the larger Kurdish, Shi'i, and Sunni camps, divisions have arisen due to kinship allegiances, political affiliations, and geography (e.g., witness the Kurdish interparty fighting of 1994–1997).

Factionalism within the provincial Sunni base poses the gravest threat to Iraq's stability. The Sunni clans from the central provinces dominate the army, the Republican Guard, and the many security organs. Consequently, they have ready access to heavy arms, training, and the military command structure. These groups are divided by feuds arising from reciprocal betrayals and by loyalties to both their kinsmen and their towns. Indeed, in order to safeguard his power, Saddam has long targeted his divide-and-rule, reward-and-punish policies directly at the core provincial Sunni communities that have supplied manpower to the military and security organs. This helps explain why the coup plots of the 1990s were hatched by groups with a narrow regional base. For example, during that decade, coups were attempted by the Jebouris, the Tikritis, the Samarris, and by Republican Guard officers from Ramadi. The narrow base for each of these plots was necessitated by fear and the need for extreme secrecy, further underlining the clans' tendency toward fragmentation and primary loyalties under pressure. Even within Saddam's tribe, the Albu Nasir, a history of assassinations and revenge killings makes cohesion doubtful in a post-Saddam Iraq.

The existence of these dangers does not mean that conflict is inevitable, for they are counterbalanced by several positive factors. First, unlike Afghanistan, Iraq does not have a history of civil war or a tradition of warlords.[2] Despite its multiple ethnicities and creeds, the country has experienced little of the intercommunal hatred and violence that have plagued similarly diverse regions (e.g., the Balkans). With few exceptions, Iraq's history of internal warfare has been characterized by hostilities between the ruling regime in Baghdad and individual communities. Therefore, a spontaneous, immediate eruption of intercommunal civil war following Saddam's removal is improbable.

Second, Iraq's civil service has a long, uninterrupted tradition of functionality, however marred it may be by corruption and cynicism. Administratively, it is at least as effective as its counterparts in other Middle Eastern countries.

Third, the Iraqi population is warweary, disillusioned, and ground down by thirty-five years of repression, twenty years of armed conflict, and twelve years of economic sanctions. Their appetite for violence is at least blunted, replaced by a desire to live free from fear and deprivation. The exhaustion of the Iraqi people and their desire for peaceful normalcy may well steer political leaders and aspirants toward less belligerent postures, which could in turn create an ideal foundation for stability. These may be minor consolations in light of the coming challenges, but they should be held squarely in view when considering the process of change in Iraq.

Meeting the Challenge

Whatever form it takes, a post-Saddam government will almost certainly be weaker than the current regime. As demonstrated in Afghanistan and other countries, wholly new governments are fragile and vulnerable to subversion. An Iraqi successor government would have to contend with dysfunctional institutions and centrifugal forces that would preclude firm control, and it would be unable to use the full coercive powers of the state to ensure the public's submission. In any case, force alone would be an insufficient tool for maintaining stability and national cohesion. In addition to cultivating power, the new government would need to cultivate legitimacy, establishing its credentials and proving its right to govern. Given these criteria, which of the three post-Saddam scenarios outlined at the beginning of this essay would have the best chance of success?

A continuity scenario that retained much of the current state structure would pose numerous problems. The organs of Saddam's regime from which a continuity government would attempt to derive its legitimacy (e.g., the RCC and the Ba'ath Party) are anathema to the vast majority of Iraqis; hence, the survival of these organs would trigger escalated resistance to a new regime throughout the country. In any case, if Saddam were no longer in power, these organs would have no independent life, and any potential leaders would lack the authority and credibility needed to win trust and acceptance from either their colleagues, the military, or the Iraqi people. None of the current members of the RCC or the Ba'ath Regional Command are likely to present a credible alternative to Saddam, nor could they survive in power unchallenged. Resistance would come from all quarters, including the military forces. Even if a Ba'ath-military alliance were formed, the civilian partners in such an arrangement would be overwhelmed in short order, leaving a military-dominated regime.

Although some may view a military regime arising from a coup as a quick and easy vehicle for change in Iraq, such a government would likely be the least conducive to stability. A military regime could perhaps use force to secure order briefly, but it would soon face strong resistance from the Kurds and Shi'is. Armed defiance and separatist tendencies in general would intensify, necessitating ever harsher military reprisals and escalating violence. Moreover, a military regime would perpetuate the militarist culture in Iraq, raising fears throughout the region. Iran in particular could become alarmed enough to intervene, perhaps by supporting Shi'i Islamist groups.

The most dire challenge to a military regime would come from the ranks of the military-security class itself. The many military, paramilitary, and security organs in Iraq have become the preserve of a select few clans from central Iraq—those promoted by Saddam since the late 1970s to serve as his power base. The competition for power among these rival groups would result in repeated challenges to a new military regime—army revolts, coups, and countercoups, all organized, as in the 1990s, by individual clans.

Indeed, if Iraq were to develop a class of warlords, it would spring from those clans that supply the top echelons of the current regime's various military and quasi-military organizations. Aside from Saddam and his family, these clans recognize no hierarchy. None can claim undisputed supremacy over the others; each regards itself as the rightful heir to power, either because of its high standing in the regime's institutions or, conversely, because of its willingness to challenge Saddam at one point or another over the past decade. As described previously, each clan also has access to some segment of the command structure and weaponry of the military-security establishment. Therefore, the logic of seizing power through force would likely prevail under a new military government, with disappointed military leaders using their power base to challenge any such regime. Iraq would then be reinfected with the disease that plagued the Arab world during the 1950s and 1960s—a constant susceptibility to military coups.

The third option for succession—a transitional unity government—would be the most likely to ensure stability. The government that succeeds Saddam's regime must draw the country together and minimize its centrifugal tendencies by attracting groups toward the center. It must give Iraq's various social and political groups a stake in the new order and a vested interest in its survival, while building a system of checks and balances through the multiplicity of interests represented within its structure. In addition to the traditional—and inherently circumscribed—ethnic and religious interests, a national unity government must tap into the urban intelligentsia and the democratic, modernizing elements of Iraqi society. Such a government would derive its legitimacy from inclusiveness and diversity, making it more likely to gain the cooperation that is essential to stability.

To gain wide credibility and support, a successor government would have to promise a new beginning for Iraq. The

Iraqi people want a government that will sweep away the corpses and ghosts of the old regime and usher in an era of democracy, participation, and rule of law. Only by making and delivering on such a promise could a national unity government ease the fears of the many groups in Iraq that are anxious about the future. The Kurds must be assured that their rights will be respected and that their gains of the past ten years will not be reversed. The Shi'is must be assured that the era of exclusion and repression is over. The Sunnis must be assured that they will not become the new victims of discrimination and reprisal. Neither a Ba'ath continuity government nor a military regime could provide such comfort to the mosaic of groups that make up Iraqi society.

Although a coalition arrangement may not produce the most efficient state structure or the strongest central authority for a post-Saddam transitional period, it would minimize the most disruptive scenarios, namely, armed dissent, military challenge, and secessionist tensions. Such a regime would therefore be best suited to steering Iraq through a fragile transition.

Besides giving Iraqis hope for a new political order, a national unity government would have the following pragmatic goals during the initial transitional period:

- dismantling the hallmark organizations of the old regime;
- establishing law and order and preventing reprisals;
- addressing the humanitarian crisis;
- beginning reconstruction of vital infrastructure;
- negotiating with the international community;
- entering into confidence-building dialogue with neighbors; and
- preparing for a constituent assembly and for the transfer of power to a constitutional government.

The principal concern of an interim government would be repairing the damage of war and putting the country back on its feet. Such a government should aim to solve immediate problems, establish a functioning civil service, protect the

Iraqi people, and maintain peace long enough to build a strong transitional bridge to a permanent constitutional arrangement.

International Assistance

The collapse of Saddam's regime will likely be swift and total, leaving behind a defunct state system. The international community must not allow a prolonged breakdown of government authority; the United States, its allies, and Iraqis themselves have a responsibility to plan the shape and functions of a successor government in advance. In the case of Afghanistan, the Bonn conference that created the interim authority in Kabul took place weeks after the start of the post–September 11 war. In Iraq's case, however, a strategy for managed change must be in place before military action is set in motion; Bonn-style thinking is needed in order to formulate, at a minimum, the basic elements of an interim government. Iraqi partners are indispensable to such planning, and the United States should take the bold step of engaging the Iraqi opposition in the process of devising systems to fill the vacuum of authority that will inevitably be created in the wake of Saddam's downfall.

Moreover, a new government in Iraq would need sustained, unstinting international assistance. Recognition, support, and economic aid from other states would enhance a new government's credibility at home and promote its stability. The international community, especially the United States, would also be responsible for ensuring that a new government had all the components necessary to lead Iraq to a better future. Simultaneously, world powers would need to assure a transitional government that regional interference in Iraq's domestic affairs would not be tolerated.

A new regime would also need to collaborate with multinational institutions and other governments in initiating a massive humanitarian and reconstruction program. Contrary to popular belief, Iraq's current revenue, after deductions for compensation and debt servicing, would be inadequate to this task. Consequently, an interim government would have to request relief through forgiveness, abatement, or rescheduling of its debt and compensation obligations, in addition to seeking new loans and investments to supplement its revenues.

A substantial program of nation building would also be needed. Most urgent, Iraq would need help rebuilding its lawmaking, law enforcement, and judicial institutions, as these are at once the most corrupt under the current regime and the most essential to a peaceful post-Saddam transition to democracy.

Simply put, a long-term international commitment to regenerating Iraqi government and society would be crucial in the wake of Saddam's ouster. Unfortunately, the post-Taliban experience in Afghanistan—where international (particularly American) engagement has thus far been limited and grudging—does not augur well. If a similar international reluctance to engage is exhibited in a post-Saddam Iraq, the consequences may well be disastrous, not only for the Iraqi people but for the entire Middle East.

Notes

1. See "The Declaration of the Shi'a of Iraq," a document signed by Shi'i expatriate leaders in July 2002. Available online (www.iraqfoundation.org/news/2002/gjuly/15_declaration_english.html). Also see the website of the declaration's framers (www.iraqishia.com).

2. The Kurdish region is an exception; there, the structure of patronage, clientage, command, allegiance, and armed militias held sway for quite some time.

Kamran Karadaghi

Minimizing Ethnic Tensions

Two contradictory views have emerged about what would happen in Iraq if Saddam Husayn were deposed. The rosy view argues that Saddam is the sole cause of Iraq's problems; therefore, all obstacles to change would disappear immediately following his ouster, and Iraqis could then begin to rebuild their country. This position is so simplistic as to be unworthy of serious discussion.

The second prospect, a gloomy view, postulates a number of negative developments. First, thousands of Sunni Arabs—particularly those in the central and western provinces of Iraq; in the towns of Tikrit, Samarra, and Ramadi; and in parts of Mosul and Baghdad—would be slaughtered by the majority Shi'i Arabs once Saddam's dreaded Republican Guard and security organizations began to collapse under a U.S.-led military attack.

Meanwhile, the Kurds would advance toward Mosul and the oil-rich city of Kirkuk, provoking a conflict with the Turkomans. Turkey would then send its troops to protect its favored group, the Turkomans, and to prevent the Kurds from conquering Kirkuk; the Turks could even annex the entire Mosul province.

At the same time, units of the Iranian Revolutionary Guards, disguised as Iraqi Islamist fighters, would cross into Iraq from the south to help their fellow Shi'is confront the remnants of Saddam's regular army and the Republican Guard, eventually gaining control over the southern and central Euphrates provinces of Iraq. The Iranians would also use Kurdish Islamist groups and elements of the Kurdistan Workers Party to destabilize northern Iraq, even intervening openly if Turkish troops entered Iraqi Kurdistan. In addition, the Iranians would quickly seize the opportunity to attack Iranian opposition groups based in Iraq (e.g., the Kurdistan Democratic Party of Iran and Mujahideen Khalq).

Although these scenarios are highly exaggerated, some degree of chaos would be inevitable in a post-Saddam Iraq, particularly as various parties settled scores and exacted revenge. Yet, neither the Iraqis, the Iranians, nor the Turks would be free to do whatever they liked in the aftermath of Saddam's removal. Rather, they would all have to take into account the presence of the American army—the likely liberator of Iraq and the primary player in determining the future of the country.

Nevertheless, the United States must be prepared to deal with each of the above scenarios as soon as the dust of regime change settles. Although the Iraqi people have no doubt that a well-planned U.S. military operation would topple Saddam quickly, most of them feel that the United States would need something beyond military might to achieve its more difficult goal of fostering fundamental change in Iraq. The difficulties that the U.S.-led coalition has faced in post-Taliban Afghanistan could be dwarfed by the potential chaos that would arise if the United States mishandled post-Saddam Iraq, reneged on its commitments, or lost political will.

To begin with, the Iraqis would have difficulty reaching a compromise agreement on the future shape of Iraq following Saddam's ouster. Only the United States is powerful enough to force compromise on them. The various Iraqi constituencies have their own agendas, none of which are likely to prove acceptable to all parties. Hence, compromise would be difficult even on widely touted ideas such as federalism. For example, the ethnicity-based federal Iraq demanded by many pro-Western Kurdish groups bears no resemblance to the territory-based federal Iraq preferred by pro-Western Iraqi Arab democrats. Moreover, both of these concepts of federalism diverge from the religious model proposed by the Islamist groups representing Iraqi Shi'i Arabs. Finally, none of these propositions are likely to satisfy the military, which insists that Iraq remain a centralized state, a perspective supported by elements among the Turkomans, Chaldeans, and Assyrians (although other elements of these groups opt for varying degrees of autonomy).

In addition, Iraqi expatriates of all persuasions have begun to engage in extensive debate about post-Saddam Iraq in anticipation of an imminent U.S. attack. For example, seminars and conferences in London and Washington have focused on Iraq's future, with ex-officers and opposition groups attempting to project a role for themselves. Moreover, prominent Shi'i exiles have adopted a "Declaration of the Shi'a of Iraq" in an unprecedented attempt to solve what many of them and their critics describe as the "Shi'i identity crisis." The Kurds, too, are openly addressing the future by offering a draft constitution for Iraq and by developing new alliances between Iraqi opposition groups.

Given all of these disparate factors, can one answer the question "What will happen after Saddam?" with any degree of certainty? Fortunately, some tentative analysis of post-Saddam Iraq is possible, particularly if one focuses on the challenge of reconstituting the Iraqi military and reconciling the divergent claims of the country's various ethnic groups.

The Military

Regardless of the agendas of Iraq's ethnic, religious, and political constituencies, the Iraqi military would be the key to managing the country both in the immediate aftermath of regime change and during the three- to five-year post-Saddam transitional period. Of course, one must draw a distinction between the regular Iraqi army and the Republican Guard. The differences between these two bodies are striking, particularly their divergent ethnic-religious structure and asymmetrical military capabilities.

The regular army ranks consist mostly of Shi'i Arab soldiers under Sunni Arab officers, who exercise control through an efficient intelligence and security system. In contrast, all of the Republican Guard's unit commanders are Sunni Arabs, along with the majority of its officers and 70–80 percent of its rank-and-file troops. Moreover, many of the Guard's leaders hail from Saddam's birthplace, Tikrit, and nearby areas. Similarly, the Special Republican Guard—the elite of the elite—is a 40,000-strong, solidly Sunni Arab army whose members hail from Baghdad and the central Sunni Arab provinces of Salahuddin, Anbar, Mosul, and Diyala. Each branch of the Republican Guard is loyal only to Saddam and his younger son Qussay, who is in charge of both corps; therefore, they can remain intact and functional even if Saddam is killed, provided Qussay survives him.

In addition, the Republican Guard is better trained and better equipped than the regular army. The Special Republican Guard has even more advanced training (e.g., in urban warfare) and can fulfill missions efficiently and swiftly, as it demonstrated in crushing the post–Gulf War Shi'i and Kurdish uprisings in 1991. In other words, even the combined forces of the regular army and Shi'i, Kurdish, and other opposition groups are no match for the two Republican Guard corps and the numerous security organizations designed by Saddam to protect his regime.

In light of the history of modern Iraq, any post-Saddam strategy that envisages handing a large degree of control to the Sunni Arab military command structure—let alone to the Republican and Special Republican Guards—would be both a nonstarter and a prelude to disaster. Conversely, a U.S. victory over the elite units could lead to the disintegration of Saddam's security services, which in turn would greatly facilitate the creation of a broad-based, civilian transitional government representing all opposition and ethnosocial groups. Such a regime could be supported by regular Iraqi army forces, on the condition that they cooperate with U.S.-led forces and submit to the control of a civilian government endorsed by the United States and the international community.

After decades of humiliation and neglect, the regular army would happily take on the task of dismantling a defeated Republican Guard and Saddam's security services. The more difficult task would come later, however, when the new government and army leadership began restructuring the armed forces and formulating a new doctrine that clearly restricted the role of the military to defending the country from outside danger.

The Sunni Arab Center

The strength of Iraq's Sunni Arab center stems from its control of both the military and the instruments of political power. Inevitably, then, the Sunni center would oppose the idea of a weakened military controlled by a civilian government that was no longer monopolized by the Sunni establishment. In negotiations on the composition of a new Iraq, these Sunnis would likely seek the support of Arab states that have grown accustomed to the Sunni Arab status quo in Iraqi government. In fact, Sunni governance has long been accepted by the United States as well, along with most other Western countries. Therefore, it would be up to the United States to achieve a breakthrough on this issue by allowing Iraqis to change the existing order following Saddam's ouster.

The Sunni center has ample cause to be anxious about life after Saddam. Not all Sunni Arabs are loyal to Saddam, but they are attached to the status quo and would cling to the privileges that come with it. Even so, the Sunni center would probably accept a new order in Iraq that allowed it to share power while striving to ensure that it remained overrepresented. These Sunnis realize that changing the balance of power in a post-Saddam Iraq would take a long time, given their decades-long dominance of Iraqi politics and their years of governmental experience. Such continuity and know-how would prove especially valuable in key sectors of post-Saddam government service, including prominent technocratic and political positions.

Outside the center, the Sunni Arab tribes would present different challenges. These tribes have played an important role in supporting Saddam's regime. Saddam has managed to create a unique system of tribal alliances, positioning his own Tikriti tribe and clan in the center. As described previously, the Republican and Special Republican Guards, along with Saddam's personal security units, have been recruited largely from Sunni tribes, which have consequently enjoyed numerous perquisites (e.g., land, money, arms). Perhaps the most distressing aspect of this ascendancy has been the Sunni tribes' tendency to foment hatred against the Shi'i tribes. Such antipathy was evident during the uprisings of 1991, when prominent Sunni Arab tribes in central Iraq, thinking Saddam's regime might fall, sent a delegation to the Kurds, who had just captured the city of Kirkuk. The Sunnis offered their cooperation on condition that the Kurds help them prevent the Shi'is from establishing an Islamic republic following a regime collapse.

Many Kurds, along with several exiled Iraqi military officers, think it unlikely that the Sunni Arab tribes would fight alongside Saddam's forces in the event of a U.S. attack. In fact, they would probably be disposed to cooperate with the Kurds again, as in 1991; after all, only a few Sunni tribes helped government forces suppress the Kurdish uprising in the Tuz Khurmatu region in Kirkuk province. Yet, the Sunni tribes are unlikely to cooperate with their fellow Arabs in the Shi'i tribes. Clearly, tribal enmities, fanned by the favoritism of Saddam's regime, would be a destabilizing element in a post-Saddam Iraq, particularly when one considers that the Sunni and Shi'i Arab tribes each have significant representation in the regular army.

The Shi'is

At a June 2002 conference in London, hundreds of prominent Shi'is—including intellectuals, professionals, academics, activists of all political stripes, community leaders (both secular and religious), and representatives of the two main Iraqi Islamic groups (the Supreme Council for Islamic Revolution in Iraq and the al-Da'wa Party)—adopted the "Declaration of the Shi'a of Iraq." This declaration asserted three basic goals: "1) The abolition of dictatorship and its replacement with democracy; 2) The abolition of ethnic discrimination and its replacement with a federal structure for Kurdistan; 3) The abolition of the policy of discrimination against the Shi'is."[1]

Iraqi Kurds have been making similar demands for years, but the June declaration was the first statement from Iraqi Shi'is dealing with issues that they had traditionally considered taboo: the genesis of the Shi'i problem; the question of Shi'i identity; the nature of the Shi'i opposition; the problem of sectarian differences and discrimination; and the Shi'i role in Iraqi national unity. The document's importance has been magnified by the fact that its framers intend to advance it as an initial negotiating position following Saddam's ouster.[2]

In general, the declaration attempts to answer a central question about post-Saddam Iraq: what do the Shi'is want? Specifically, it stresses the importance of civil rights that "have a special resonance for the Shi'is." These rights (which likely reflect the expectations of the majority of the Shi'i population) include the following:

1. Their right to practice their own religious rites and rituals and to autonomously administer their own religious shrines and institutions, through legitimate Shi'i religious authorities;
2. Full freedom to conduct their religious affairs in their own mosques, meeting halls and other institutions;
3. Freedom to teach in their religious universities and institutions with no interference by the central or provincial authorities;
4. Freedom of movement and travel and assembly on the part of the higher Shi'i religious authorities, *ulema,* and speakers, and guarantees afforded to the teaching circles—the *hawzas*—to conduct their affairs in a manner that they see fit;
5. Ensuring that the Shi'i religious shrines and cities are entered into UNESCO's World Heritage Sites and are thus protected from arbitrary acts of change and destruction;
6. Full freedoms to publish Shi'i tracts and books and to establish Shi'i religious institutions and assemblies;
7. The right to establish independent schools, universities, and other teaching establishments and academies, within the framework of a broad and consensual national education policy;

8. Introduction of the elements of the *Jafari* creed and rites into the national educational curriculum, in a manner similar to the way in which other schools of Islamic jurisprudence are taught;
9. Revising the elements of the history curriculum to remove all disparagement of the Shi'is, and the writing of an authentic history that would remove any anti-Shi'a biases;
10. Freedom to establish Shi'i mosques, meeting halls, and libraries;
11. Respect for the burial grounds of the Shi'is;
12. Official recognition by the state of the key dates of the Shi'i calendar;
13. Repatriation of all Iraqis who were forcibly expelled from Iraq, or who felt obliged to leave under duress, and the full restitution of their constitutional and civil rights.[3]

The Sunni Arab establishment in Iraq—under whom the Shi'is have been subjected to unimaginable brutality, discrimination, and injustice—will find some of these demands hard to digest. In general, though, there is no reason to think that such demands could not be met in a post-Saddam Iraq.

The most difficult obstacle would be political representation. Shi'is make up 60–65 percent of the Iraqi population as a whole and 85 percent of the Arab population, but their underrepresentation in the institutions of power is striking. For example, fewer than 5 percent of the country's approximately 500 military generals are Shi'is. Obviously, the Shi'is would demand proportional representation in the political structure of a post-Saddam Iraq, as well as an immediate end to the injustices they have suffered. Yet, as one prominent Shi'i political activist stated, it would be "impossible to jump overnight from nil to 60–65 percent representation."[4]

Presumably, then, the Shi'is would not adopt a position of maximal demands. From a practical standpoint, the Shi'is could settle for a formula of political representation based on the following percentages: 30-30-30-10 for, respectively, Shi'is, Sunnis, Kurds, and other groups (e.g., Turkomans, Chaldeans, and Assyrians). Some of the signatories to the Shi'i declaration have indicated that a 25-25-25-25 arrangement would be acceptable, arguing that such a formula would guarantee sociopolitical balance and minimize ethnic-sectarian conflict. The Shi'is would probably count on the Kurds to support them in this position (Faili Kurds feel equally strong affiliations with Kurds and Shi'is), as well as the Turkomans (40 percent of whom are Shi'i), the Chaldeans, and the Assyrians. Such support may well be forthcoming, considering that the Ba'ath regime deported hundreds of thousands of Faili Kurds and Shi'i Turkomans to Iran during the 1970s and 1980s.

Nevertheless, the Shi'is would feel vulnerable in the immediate aftermath of Saddam's ouster and may therefore seek the protection of a guarantor state. Because no regional state would be willing to provide such protection, this role would likely fall to the United States; even Shi'i Islamic political groups would subscribe to this arrangement, assuming they had freed themselves of Iranian influence beforehand.

The Kurds

Thanks to the de facto state that they have been able to sustain in northern Iraq for the past ten years, the Kurds have a level of organization and governmental experience that is unique among the Iraqi opposition. Therefore, they would be one of the key players in a post-Saddam Iraq, with a particularly strong negotiating position. Given this advantage, the two main Iraqi Kurdish groups—the Patriotic Union of Kurdistan (PUK) and the Kurdistan Democratic Party (KDP)—would be unlikely to relinquish their demand for a federal state following Saddam's removal. Moreover, many smaller Kurdish parties would likely follow their lead on this issue, along with a majority of the Kurdish tribes. Even pro-Baghdad Kurdish tribes would return to the mainstream Kurdish fold if a civilian government emerged to lead post-Saddam Iraq. (If a military regime assumed power, however, they would seek its protection.) In addition, the Kurds believe that the majority of Iraq's Assyrian and Chaldean populations would join the mainstream Kurdish movement in the hopes of gaining more rights within the Kurdish portion of a federal state.

Yet, the Kurdish Islamist groups would not be so quick to fall in line. They are, and will remain, under Iran's control; therefore, they constitute the main instrument by which Tehran would seek to influence (or simply destabilize) post-Saddam northern Iraq in order to serve Iranian interests.

Many Turkomans would also be wary about the possibility of a federal Iraq in which Kurds ruled the north. In particular, the Turkoman Front, which enjoys the support of Turkey, may well challenge the Kurdish mainstream. Given Turkey's presumably prominent role in any U.S.-led coalition to remove Saddam, the Turkoman Front would likely demand its own say in the fate of Iraqi Kurdistan.

Two factors may persuade the Kurds to maintain a reasonably united position. First, both of the main Kurdish parties would face significant pressure from other groups in a new post-Saddam government. Second, many Kurds would view the presence of American forces as a kind of safeguard against widespread loss of control, minimizing the risks of insisting on a federal state.

Federalism need not be a divisive issue; although various Iraqi constituencies have differing interpretations of federalism, the idea of a federal Iraq is becoming a common denominator among many groups. As described previously, however, disagreement would emerge if the Kurds insisted on an ethnicity-based federal arrangement. Both the PUK and the KDP seem to be aware of this sticking point; recently, they have stated publicly that their concept of federalism is based on geographic-administrative rather than ethnic-nationalistic parameters. Interestingly enough, this position echoes one of the platforms in the "Declaration of the Shi'a of Iraq": "Iraq's federal structure would not be based on a sectarian division but rather on administrative and demographic criteria."

Kirkuk is another potentially divisive issue in the debate about federalism. Specifically, the Kurds may insist on full control over Kirkuk in a federal Iraqi Kurdistan. Such a demand would be perceived as a forerunner of complete secession from Iraq, since the oil-rich province could provide the economic means for a viable independent state. For decades, both the Iraqi army and the Sunni Arab establishment have been told that the regime's endless anti-Kurdish military campaigns were waged in order to prevent the Kurds from controlling Kirkuk and, in turn, seceding from Iraq. Changing this mentality overnight would be impossible, and the Kurds would risk losing a great deal if they failed to address the issue of Kirkuk appropriately. Provided they maintained their unity, the Kurds could reach an agreement on an attainable concept of federalism based on ethnic, territorial, and administrative principles, perhaps with a special status for Kirkuk. The military would find such a solution acceptable.

In any case, the Kurds have a strong incentive to seek the establishment of a democratic regime in Baghdad, one that grants them a bigger role in the political and economic decisionmaking process. If the Iraqis failed to reach a compromise agreement on a post-Saddam federal structure, the Kurds would be forced into an isolated position, which would in turn open the door for Iranian and Turkish interference.

Iran and Turkey

Both Tehran and Ankara would go to great lengths to ensure that regime change in Iraq did not threaten their interests. Iran, for one, does not want a democratic, pro-Western regime in Baghdad. Moreover, Tehran fears that the United States might make Iran—part of President George W. Bush's "axis of evil"—its next target after Saddam. Iran would therefore seek to influence post-Saddam Iraq through local alliances, stopping short of direct military interference. In the north, the Iranians would increase their support of extreme Islamic groups such as Ansar al-Islam and other "Kurdish Afghans" who are allegedly linked with Osama bin Laden's al-Qaeda. Mainstream Kurdish Islamic groups could fall under Tehran's sway as well. Currently, the PUK and KDP authorities are forced to tolerate these groups in order to please Iran; however, such groups may come to fear that they would lose their privileges in the Kurdish status quo in a post-Saddam federal state. Unlike southern Iraq—where the borders with Iran could be controlled by a U.S.-led force or by the Iraqi army—the mountainous terrain in Iraqi Kurdistan would make it easy for Tehran to continue manipulating the Kurds.

Turkey's main concern is the potential emergence of a Kurdish state in northern Iraq. The Turks would have a stronger hand than the Iranians, considering that they would likely take part in a U.S.-led coalition to overthrow Saddam. The Kurds would be alarmed by any Turkish move, particularly a military one. They would feel less threatened if the Turks entered Kurdish territory as part of a coalition force under U.S. command, in which case the Kurds would be obliged to cooperate.

A unilateral Turkish military advance into northern Iraq, however, would increase tension on two fronts: Kurdish-Turkish and Kurdish-Turkoman. In fact, the Kurds and Turkomans would be at odds even in the absence of a Turkish military presence. The Turkomans have expressed serious grievances over their maltreatment by the majority Kurds in the north and are increasingly demanding autonomy, along with recognition of Kirkuk as a Turkoman-majority city. The Turkomans are strongly opposed to the notion of a Kurdish federal state within Iraq. For their part, the Kurds regard Turkoman claims as pretexts for Turkish interference.

All in all, Turks, Kurds, and Turkomans alike seem to be in an uncompromising mood regarding these issues. Both Kurds and Turkomans could therefore be expected to seek support from allies in the event of regime change. The Turkomans would appeal mainly to Turkey. The Turks would in turn play the Turkoman card in order to pressure the United States, in the hope of offsetting Kurdish demands.

Conclusion

In light of all of the above factors, several conclusions can be drawn about any attempts to remake Iraq. First, regime change would presumably take place as a result of a U.S.-led military operation, one that included the dismantling of the elite Republican and Special Republican Guards and Saddam's security apparatus. This would clear the way for the regular army to play a positive role: enforcing security and stability under the control of a new civilian government.

Second, in the aftermath of Saddam's ouster, a degree of anarchy may obtain for a short period, during which time violent acts of revenge would likely take place. Such acts would not be carried out on a grand scale, however, and would be limited to certain parts of the country. The presence of U.S.-led forces in Iraq would ensure a quick end to any such chaos.

The U.S. presence would also be conducive to a negotiating atmosphere in which Iraqi constituencies could reach a relatively fair compromise agreement on power sharing. For the foreseeable future, the Sunni Arabs would continue to be overrepresented in the new order, and the Shi'is underrepresented. The Kurds would strive to secure a larger role in Baghdad, but they would face difficulties in their relations with the Turkomans, Turkey, and Iran.

Finally, owing to the disparate agendas of the main political, ethnic, and sectarian groups, the restructuring of Iraq would take a long time. Additional problems would arise from the attempts of neighboring states, particularly Turkey and Iran, to interfere in post-Saddam Iraq, either directly or through their local allies in various parts of the country. To prevent Iraq from careening out of control, U.S.-led forces would be required to remain in the country for as long as it took to ensure the establishment of a stable, capable government.

Notes

1. The text of the declaration is available online in both English and Arabic; see the website created by the framers (www.iraqishia.com).

2. According to information obtained in the author's July 23, 2002, telephone interview with one of the framers.

3. "Declaration of the Shi'a of Iraq."

4. Interview, July 23, 2002.

Michael Rubin

Federalism and the Future of Iraq

The Ba'ath Party has ruled Iraq with an iron fist for almost thirty-five years. When the day comes that Saddam Husayn no longer holds power, a deep reconstruction of the Iraqi state and society will be required, both to maintain order and to allow a viable Iraq to rejoin the international community. The question of what happens to Iraq under a new regime cannot be shunted aside, especially as fear of the alternative dominates discussion among those opposed to regime change.

In fact, a model already exists for a post-Saddam Iraq. For the past decade, three-and-a-half Kurdish-administered governorates in northern Iraq have not only been effectively free of Saddam's control, but have thrived in comparison to the rest of Iraq. The success of Iraqi Kurdistan provides a model for post-Saddam reconstruction: a federalist structure with locally autonomous regions, all presided over by a weak central government in Baghdad that would still control defense, foreign affairs, oil, and national infrastructure. Although some Kurds talk about a tripartite federalism splitting Iraq into Shi'i Arab, Sunni Arab, and Kurdish states, such a division would be unacceptable to most parties. Yet, a federalism based on administrative divisions rather than ethnicity or religion would best ensure stability in post-Saddam Iraq.

Background on the Federalist Model

Federalism is not a new concept for Iraq. Prior to the Ottoman Empire's defeat in World War I, the area that would eventually become Iraq consisted of three separate Ottoman provinces: Basra in the south, Baghdad in the center, and Mosul in the north. Even after the 1921 establishment of the Iraqi monarchy, the final shape of Iraq remained in dispute as the nascent Turkish Republic laid claim to Mosul. In 1925, a League of Nations commission arrived to adjudicate the dispute; they found in favor of Iraq, awarding the predominantly Kurdish province to the new government in Baghdad under the following conditions: "Regard must be paid to the desires expressed by the Kurds that officials of Kurdish race should be appointed for the administration of their country, the dispensation of justice, and teaching in the schools, and that Kurdish should be the official language of all these services."[1]

Successive governments in Baghdad failed to implement this autonomy. Although sporadic outbreaks of ethnic violence had occurred throughout Iraqi history, a full-scale Kurdish revolt erupted in 1961. Following the Ba'ath Party coup in 1968, the new Iraqi government announced its intention to grant the rebellious Kurds a measure of autonomy. Saddam Husayn—then the vice chairman of the ruling Revolutionary Command Council—took charge of these negotiations, which culminated in a March 11, 1970, agreement that promised Kurdish language rights, the appointment of a Kurdish vice president, appointments to high-level cabinet and military posts, economic development for Iraqi Kurdistan, and proportionate legislative representation. Yet, disputes over the delimitation of Kurdistan (namely, whether Kirkuk should be included), as well as Saddam's own efforts to undermine the accords as the Ba'ath Party consolidated control, caused the collapse of Arab-Kurdish federalism and the resumption of low-intensity civil war. Nevertheless, the willingness of the Iraqi government to embrace federalism has remained in the collective memory of the Iraqi people.

Federalism in Practice: The Kurdish Safe Haven

Iraqi Kurdish history following the collapse of the autonomy accords is well known. During the late 1980s, Kurdish-populated northern Iraq was the scene of near total destruction, the Iraqi government having devastated more than 4,000 of the 4,655 Kurdish villages.[2] In October 1991, Saddam Husayn, unable to reach a political accord with Iraq's Kurds or to counter the resurgence of Kurdish guerrilla activity, ordered a food and fuel blockade of Iraqi Kurdistan and withdrew his government's administration from the area. Almost overnight, the area of de facto Kurdish control expanded from 3,600 square miles in the safe haven around Zakho and Dahuk to a crescent-shaped 15,500-square-mile swath of territory stretching from the Syrian border, across the entire length of the Turkish frontier, and southward along the Iranian border, some 200 miles below the no-fly zone.

The Iraqi government's blockade caused infant and even adult mortality rates to skyrocket in the north. Many doctors have pointed out that children born during the so-called "starving winter" of 1991–1992 have abnormally low rates of growth. Moreover, few forests in the area are more than a decade old because most of the trees were cut for firewood during those difficult months.

Only a decade later, however, the towns and cities of Iraqi Kurdistan stand transformed, illustrating that a change in governance can drastically alter quality of life, and suggesting that post-Saddam reconstruction and development will be far easier than the worst-case scenarios being bandied about on Capitol Hill and in the press, which describe a twenty-year, multibillion-dollar U.S. commitment to reconstruction. Given power to allocate funds locally, Iraqi Kurds have turned a neglected wasteland into relative affluence. As a result, infant mortality has declined and fertility has increased. The region as a whole has emerged from years of authoritarian dictatorship, low-intensity conflict, brutal police actions, and corruption to host the most vibrant economy within Iraq.

For example, on the former site of the Ba'ath Party's Dahuk headquarters and prison now stands the University of Dahuk. The former Republican Guard base has been replaced by the Mazi supermarket, where locals shop for Italian designer clothing, Japanese electronics, Turkish canned goods, and local produce, their purchases totaled by infrared scanners at the checkout counters. Irbil, the capital of the

Kurdistan Regional Government (or at least of the Kurdistan Democratic Party [KDP] sector), is now a city of more than one million inhabitants, boasting new hotels, parks, and schools. The former Iraqi military camp in the center of Sulaymaniyah is now called Freedom Park and includes a duck pond, restaurant, indoor swimming pool, and even a botanical maze. The nearby Shaykh Mahmud mosque is decorated in Kurdish colors and motifs. The Ba'ath Party security prison in Sulaymaniyah, still bullet-pocked, stands as a monument to the victims of Saddam Husayn. Other monuments, constructed from the shells of chemical ordnance, stand in Halabja, site of the Iraqi government's chemical bombardment in 1988 that killed 5,000 civilians. In short, the relative success of Iraqi Kurdistan provides a case study of how Iraq can rebuild and redefine itself once free of the yoke of Ba'ath Party dictatorship. This success also illustrates why federalism should be based on smaller administrative units rather than on larger conceptions of ethnicity or religion.

In the vacuum created by Saddam's withdrawal of Ba'ath administrative organs, the Kurds also scrambled to create a political authority. They did so largely by democratic means, despite their reputation for engaging in factional and tribal squabbles. In May 1992 elections, the KDP took 45 percent of the vote, while the rival Patriotic Union of Kurdistan (PUK) won 44 percent. The remaining votes went to the Islamic Movement, the Kurdistan Socialist Party, the Iraqi Communist Party, and the Kurdistan Popular Democratic Party (the Turkoman minority did not participate). Masud Barzani and Jalal Talebani agreed to share power in what would thereafter be known as the Kurdistan Regional Government. In the 105-member Kurdistan National Assembly, the KDP and PUK each won fifty seats, while Assyrian Christian groups occupied the remaining five. All KDP ministers and governors had PUK deputies, and vice versa.

Political development was not smooth, though. The governing coalition began to unravel in May 1994, when a land dispute in the small town of Qaladiza escalated into factional battles across the Kurdish region. The PUK seized sole control of Irbil, accusing their KDP colleagues of embezzling revenue from the lucrative Ibrahim Khalil (or Habur) customs post on the Turkish border. This dispute, which led to significant bloodshed, illustrates the need for financial transparency in a post-Saddam Iraqi government.

Further bloodshed erupted in August 1996, when the KDP cooperated with the Iraqi Republican Guard to sweep into Irbil and beyond, driving the PUK into Iran. The Republican Guard withdrew after several days, but a renewed PUK offensive virtually divided northern Iraq.[3]

Today, northern Iraq continues to be effectively divided into two rival zones, bypassing the artificial need for ethnic unity. The KDP administers the northwestern Dahuk province and all but a small slice of the north-central Irbil province. The PUK administers the northeastern Sulaymaniyah province, the northern portion of the Kirkuk (or Ta'mim) province, and the area around Kuysanjaq in the Irbil province.

Yet, high unemployment and even greater underemployment persist in the north, as does a tendency toward personality cults, especially in KDP-administered regions. In May 2001, for example, the principal of the Layla Qassim High School in Dahuk had in her small office four pictures of Masud Barzani, two photos of Masud's nephew, Prime Minister Nechervan Barzani, and two framed portraits of the KDP's founder, Mulla Mustafa al-Barzani. Masud and Nechervan Barzani have constructed and occupied a huge complex of buildings in Salahuddin; it remains unclear whether the former resort is now the property of the local government, the KDP, or the Barzanis. Abuse of power and political patronage remain serious issues in both PUK and KDP territory.

Post-Saddam Federalism

The two de facto states—PUK and KDP—in the area of Kurdish control provide a model of how a future federal Iraq might operate. Although numerous commentators deride the Iraqi Kurds for their lack of unity, Iraq's Kurds, Sunni Arabs, and Shi'i Arabs need not speak with one voice in order to form well-functioning societies. Civilians in both the PUK and

KDP portions of northern Iraq have suggested that life im-
proved after the PUK-KDP civil war because of ensuing
competition between the parties to win the hearts and
minds of their constituents. One explained, "When the
[PUK and KDP] government was unified, nothing hap-
pened. Now the KDP builds playgrounds, so the PUK rushes
to catch up. The PUK builds internet cafes, and suddenly
the KDP follows."[4]

Similarly, fears that federalism might lead to separatism
are misplaced. Administrative federalism involves only devo-
lution of power to each of Iraq's eighteen provinces, keeping
the power of the Kurds, Shi'is, and Sunnis in balance and
preventing the domination of any minority on a national level.
A weak central government would retain power over defense and foreign policy.

The fundamental economic structure of federalism in
Iraq—in the form of United Nations (UN) Security Council
Resolution 986, the oil-for-food program—is already six years
old. Adopted by the Security Council on April 14, 1995
(though not implemented for more than a year because of
Baghdad's objections), the program uses the proceeds of Iraqi
oil sales to purchase food and medicine as well as to repair
vital infrastructure. The program has profoundly reshaped
Kurdish-controlled northern Iraq, and its functioning dem-
onstrates how Iraqi national resources might be distributed
among federal regions in a post-Saddam Iraq.

The UN divides the revenue from Iraqi oil sales as follows: 72 percent to the humanitarian program, 25 percent to
the compensation committee, and the remainder to cover
UN administrative costs. Although Baghdad controls the
program's implementation in the 90 percent of the country
that it controls, the UN implements the humanitarian programs in the Kurdish-controlled north, allocating 13 percent
of oil revenues for the region, a figure proportional to the
northern governorates' population. Presumably, in the future,
each province would receive its population's share of oil revenue; money would be distributed on a regional rather than
a communal basis. Speaking in August 2001, Barham Salih,

prime minister of the PUK, called the oil-for-food program "truly revolutionary" in that "never in our history did we have a government obliged by international law to devote Iraq's oil revenues to the well-being of the Iraqi people."[5]

Whatever system of government is established in a post-Saddam Iraq, the question of oil money will have to be addressed. The sums are substantive. According to statistics released by the UN's Office of the Iraq Program,[6] between December 10, 1996 (when Iraq began to export oil under the terms of the program), and January 25, 2002, more than $50 billion flowed into oil-for-food accounts, a sum far higher than initially envisioned—both because of the lifting of caps on Iraqi oil exports and a rise in world oil prices.

Separatism or Stability?

Again, a major fear concerning federalism is that it might catalyze separatism in Iraq and plunge the region into chaos. By this logic, the formalizing of Kurdish autonomy might encourage the Kurds to declare their independence, leading to unrest in neighboring Turkey, Iran, and Syria. Likewise, Iran, in an attempt to diminish the threat from its historic rival, might encourage the Iraqi Shi'is to separate and form an Islamist rump state.

Notwithstanding the importance of such concerns, federalism may actually be the best mechanism for maintaining Iraq's stability. After all, high-profit national resources can often become the subject of territorial fights. In Liberia, successive groups and governments have fought to monopolize the nation's diamond mines. In Angola, the government and the oppositionist National Union for the Total Independence of Angola (UNITA) competed for control of the oil fields. In Afghanistan, where no ethnic group forms a majority, successive ethnically or tribally based warlords have sought to win control of Kabul, not only in pursuit of personal power, but also so that their constituents would not be marginalized in the division of international aid and state resources.

In Iraq, oil is the largest source of income. The Kirkuk oil field was Iraq's first major strike, although its production has been in decline for years. Nevertheless, this field remains a potential prize for Iraqi Kurds, Turkomans, or Arabs eager to exploit its substantial remaining reserves. Much more substantial are the oil fields at Majnun and al-Rumaylah in predominantly Shi'i southern Iraq. If Saddam is replaced by a strong centralized—as opposed to federal—government, traditionally marginalized Iraqi groups such as the Kurds, Turkomans, or Shi'is may determine that it is in their interests to fight for control of the oil fields.

In contrast, a federal system could allocate common resources according to the proportion of the population in each district, greatly reducing both the incentive to fight and communal vulnerability. Potentially tricky disputes, such as that between Kurds and Turkomans over Kirkuk, can best be sidestepped or at least contained by basing federalism on smaller, administrative units, such as the existing eighteen provinces.

Apart from equitable division of resources, other factors suggest that the separatist threat in Iraq has been exaggerated. For example, during the past decade of effective Kurdish self-rule in northern Iraq, the school curriculum has been altered only slightly. Indeed, the presidents of all three universities in Iraqi Kurdistan continue to conform largely to the national curriculum set by Iraq's Ministry of Education, despite the fact that Baghdad banned admittance of those living in the northern governorates to universities operating in regions of Ba'ath control. Even in primary and secondary schools (especially in the KDP-controlled areas), standard Iraqi textbooks are used, although teachers instruct children to tear out pictures of Saddam. Arabic continues to dominate in Dahuk, but Kurdish (the Sorani dialect, written in a modified Arabic alphabet) is the primary language of instruction in Sulaymaniyah. The growing dominance of Kurdish, especially in Sulaymaniyah, is a double-edged sword: the growing linguistic divide reinforces the case for Iraqi federalism, but incompetence in Arabic will diminish the contribution Kurds can make to any national civil service in the post-Saddam era.

Iraqi Federalism and Regional Security

Turkey is greatly concerned about Kurdish autonomy in northern Iraq, and Ankara advocates a strong central government in Baghdad to reduce any separatist threat. U.S. policymakers must regard Turkey's security as paramount. Turkey has been a steadfast American ally for more than half a century and put itself at grave risk during the Cold War as a NATO frontline state. American policymakers have an unfortunate tendency of coddling adversaries in the name of engagement while bullying allies into adopting positions contrary to their democratic mandate. Clearly, though, a federalized Iraq would be more likely to guarantee Turkish security than would a strong, centralized Iraqi state.

Iraq's Kurds have been autonomous for a decade. As their economic success has grown under the oil-for-food program, Kurdish nationalist rhetoric has declined. Universities and government offices throughout Iraqi Kurdistan still mark Iraqi army day as an official holiday. Although many hotels and government offices fly the Kurdish regional flag, the Kurdish parliament in Irbil passed a law in early 2001 that called for flying the Iraqi flag higher than the Kurdish flag as soon as Baghdad ratifies a federal structure for Iraq. The Kurdish region continues to use the Iraqi dinar, albeit an older issue of the currency than that which is used in Baghdad. Local law is based entirely on the Iraqi legal code, with only minor modifications regarding the allowance of political plurality and mitigation of the severity of many punishments. Many outsiders see Kurdish nationalist claims as homogeneous, but there is marked antipathy between the Iraqi Kurdish groups and the Turkish Kurdistan Workers Party (PKK). Neither Barzani nor Talebani subscribes to the PKK's Marxist rhetoric, nor do they seek political unity with Turkish Kurds, who far outnumber Iraqi Kurds.

Yet, the trauma of Saddam's violence against the Kurds should not be underestimated (e.g., al-Anfal [The spoils], the 1988 ethnic cleansing campaign in which Saddam razed villages and killed more than 100,000 ethnic Kurds; the various Saddam-directed chemical weapons attacks against the

Kurdish population). After the slaughter that occurred in the 1980s and their taste of autonomy in the 1990s, most Iraqi Kurds insist that they are not willing to risk the guarantees of even the most benevolent centralized successor regime. Should an Arab-dominated government in Baghdad seek to reimpose direct rule on the Dahuk, Irbil, and Sulaymaniyah provinces, Kurdish residents have said that they would revert to guerrilla war, a development that would only bolster the PKK.

The KDP, which controls the entire Iraqi-Turkish frontier, has maintained greater control over the border during the past decade than did the government in Baghdad during the ten years previous to the establishment of the safe haven. Neither U.S. nor Turkish policymakers wish to see the security now prevalent along Iraq's frontier with Turkey undermined in a way that could reverse progress made in the fight against the PKK, encourage Iranian inroads, or create a vacuum in which drug smuggling could flourish. Turkey fears not only Kurdish nationalism, but also the prospect of another Lebanon or Afghanistan emerging on its borders. If Ankara had to choose between these two fears, nationalism would be far easier to tolerate. In fact, an increasingly strong minority within Turkish military and political circles quietly argues that the de facto Kurdish entity in northern Iraq has not had the negative effects on the Kurdish situation in Turkey that many had predicted. (This position is not held by the majority of the Turkish general staff, however, nor is it officially acknowledged by the Turkish Foreign Ministry.)

Kuwait and Saudi Arabia likewise are not averse to Iraqi federalism as long as it poses no danger to Iraq's territorial integrity. The greatest concern of these Arab neighbors is Iranian infiltration into southern Iraq. Yet, significant ethnic friction persists between Persian and Arab Shi'is, despite common religious sentiment. Moreover, during the eight-year Iran-Iraq War, there were no mass defections of Iraqi Shi'is to the Iranian side. In any event, a federal Iraq would be less likely to pose an offensive military threat to its neighbors. In

1995, King Hussein of Jordan told an American audience that a federal solution to Iraq would be "optimal," a view shared by his brother, Prince Hassan, who is increasingly involved in Iraqi affairs.[7]

Most important, Iraqi Arabs—both Shi'i and Sunni—also endorse federalism. In 1996, Ayatollah Muhammad Baqir al-Hakim, leader of the Shi'i and pro-Iranian Supreme Council for Islamic Revolution in Iraq, endorsed federalism so long as it was not based on sectarian divisions. Both Mudar Shawkat, leader of the predominantly Sunni Arab Iraqi National Movement, and Ahmad Chalabi, leader of the broader Iraqi National Congress, concur.[8]

Conclusion

Although Washington must act unilaterally, if necessary, to protect itself from a growing Iraqi threat to American security, the shape and stability of a post-Saddam Iraq are regional concerns. Jordan, Turkey, and Kuwait are strong American allies, and post-Saddam Iraq must not pose a threat to them, directly or indirectly. For almost half a century, Iraq has been governed by a series of strongmen who have sought to impose increasingly autocratic control. In addition to causing an economic disaster, this strategy has essentially backfired; although Saddam tightened his grip on southern and central Iraq, he was unable to maintain effective control over northern Iraq. Only after the Kurdish uprising and the establishment of the safe haven did a tenuous stability return to the region.

Kurdish autonomy may have been accidental, but it has worked. Devolved power has resulted in an economic boom and has also effectively ended the civil insurrection that existed almost continuously from 1961 to 1991. As Kurds increasingly recognize the benefits of remaining part of Iraq, separatist rhetoric has declined. Moreover, as the Iraqi Kurdish economy flourishes, both the PUK and KDP recognize that they have too much to lose by supporting the PKK or other separatist movements. If regional stability and the maintenance of Iraq's territorial integrity are the desired ends of a post-Saddam regime, then federalism, not central control, is the most effective means.

Notes

1. League of Nations, *Report submitted to the Council by the Commission instituted by the Council Resolution of September 30, 1924,* Document C.400, M.147, vii (Geneva, 1925), as cited in David McDowall, *A Modern History of the Kurds* (London: I. B. Tauris, 1996), pp. 145–46.

2. Michael Rubin, "Interview: Nasreen Mustafa Sideek [minister of reconstruction and development for the Kurdistan Regional Government in northern Iraq]," *Middle East Intelligence Bulletin* 3, no. 7 (July 2001). Also available online (www.meib.org/articles/0107_iri.htm).

3. Patrick Cockburn, "Secret War: As Kurds Fight over a Road, Saddam Tightens His Grip," *Independent* (London), November 13, 1997. This information was corroborated by interviews with military surgeons who served during the conflict.

4. Personal communication.

5. Author's interview with Salih via internet connection between Sulaymaniyah, Iraq, and Washington, D.C., August 18, 2001.

6. This office maintains a running tally of Iraqi oil-for-food income. The periodically updated statistics are available online (www.un.org/Depts/oip/background/basicfigures.html).

7. David Makovsky, "Hussein: Divide Iraq along Ethnic Lines," *Jerusalem Post,* November 1, 1995.

8. *Al-Hayat,* April 1, 1996. See also *al-Hayat,* July 26, 2002.

Safwat Rashid Sidqi
A Criminal Regime: Accountability in a Post-Saddam Iraq

The crimes committed against the Iraqi people by their own government are so grave that describing them as "abuses" or "human rights violations" is not only a gross understatement, but an injustice to the victims and their families. These crimes far exceed the typical rights violations committed by repressive regimes (e.g., intimidating voters at the ballot box, cracking down on peaceful demonstrations, or interrogating detainees without an attorney present). The actions taken against the Iraqi people in general, and the Kurds in particular, are so inhuman and so vast in dimension as to be unprecedented in modern history.

In addition to victimizing Iraqis, Saddam Husayn's regime has committed crimes against neighboring countries, including crimes against peace (in the invasions of Iran and Kuwait), war crimes (in executing prisoners of war and using chemical weapons against Iranian soldiers during the Iran-Iraq War), and crimes against humanity (in the actions of the Iraqi regime and armed forces toward the people of Kuwait and Iran). If the process of national reconciliation in a post-Saddam Iraq is to succeed, the perpetrators of such atrocities must be held accountable.

A full discussion of the Iraqi regime's record of crime is beyond the scope of this essay. Nevertheless, it is essential that the outside world, along with many unknowing Iraqis, be informed about the behavior of the oppressive regime under which the Iraqi people have lived for the past thirty-four years.

The Record of Saddam's Regime

After seizing control of Iraq in a 1968 coup, the Ba'ath regime gradually stepped up its repressive criminal activities, climaxing internally with various genocide campaigns, described below, and externally with aggressive wars against neighboring states. Saddam Husayn in particular has ruled with an iron fist since assuming power in 1979, using limitless, unrestricted authority and the vast wealth of Iraq to achieve his goals.

During the course of his rule, Saddam has created a security apparatus consisting of more than 400,000 agents. This apparatus was not designed to ensure the safety of the Iraqi people. On the contrary, its function is to protect the regime from reprisals by suppressing and controlling would-be adversaries and the population at large. To fulfill this purpose, the security forces have been given all-inclusive powers to arrest whomever they suspect of wrongdoing, to carry out illegal interrogations, and to extract false confessions through the use of savage methods. Some Iraqi experts estimate that the security forces have perfected some one hundred types of torture. For example, many victims have been handcuffed behind their backs and hung by their arms, shocked in their genitals, jabbed with bottles and other hard objects, and/or raped in front of their family members.

Yet, the worst crime committed by Saddam's regime has been genocide. The United Nations (UN) Convention on the Prevention and Punishment of the Crime of Genocide defines genocide as

> any of the following acts committed with intent to destroy, in whole or in part, a national, ethnic, racial or religious group, as such: a) Killing members of the group; b) Causing serious bodily or mental harm to members of the group; c) Deliberately inflicting on the group conditions of life calculated to bring about its physical destruction in whole or in part; d) Imposing measures intended to prevent births within the group; e) Forcibly transferring children of the group to another group.[1]

By this definition, the Iraqi regime is liable for several acts of genocide.

The regime's most comprehensive attempt at genocide was perhaps the al-Anfal campaign. Al-Anfal (The spoils) was the official code name of a series of military operations that Saddam carried out between February and September 1988 against Iraqi Kurds, resulting in the deaths of thousands of noncombatant Kurdish citizens.[2] The forces employed in the campaign included the Kurdish *jash* troops, who were on the payroll of the Iraqi army and numbered more than 250,000 combatants; these forces were backed by armored divisions, heavy artillery units, fighters, bombers, and helicopter gunships using chemical and conventional weapons. The aims of the campaign, its huge scale, the methods used, the indiscriminate targeting of an entire civilian population, the destruction of the rural economy and infrastructure, and the designation of the affected area as a "prohibited region" all constitute indisputable evidence of genocide.

The results of the campaign included the elimination of more than 2,000 Kurdish villages in Iraqi Kurdistan (in addition to the 2,000 Turkoman and Assyrian villages destroyed there previously), along with the enforced disappearance of more than 100,000 unarmed civilians, including women, children, and the elderly. Some reports suggested that these civilians were buried alive in ditches in southern Iraq.

Other acts of genocide committed by Saddam's regime include the following:

- More than 250,000 Faili (Shi'i) Kurdish families and more than 100,000 Arab families were deported by the regime in April 1980. Forced across the border into Iran after a sudden roundup, the deportees had only the clothes on their backs and the money they were carrying in their pockets.
- One night in 1983, Iraqi intelligence agents rounded up approximately 8,000 men of the Barzani tribe from their enforced residence in Qushtappa village near Irbil. The men were loaded into gray buses and trans-

ported to southern Iraq, where they disappeared without a trace.[3]

- An estimated 20 million landmines were laid at random and without maps in Iraqi Kurdistan during the Iran-Iraq War. They were often dispersed in agricultural and other noncombat areas in order to render them uninhabitable.[4]

- The regime has used chemical weapons against its own citizens in the town of Halabja and in hundreds of villages in the Sulaymaniyah, Garmian, and Badinan areas of Iraqi Kurdistan. Five thousand civilians, most of them women, children, and the elderly, were killed in the 1988 Halabja attack alone. Moreover, in the years since these attacks, hundreds of cases of congenital abnormalities and unique cancers have been reported.

- The Third River Project was accelerated in the early 1990s in order to dry up the southern marshes and make them uninhabitable. The regime also ordered the mass killing of the Ma'dan, or Marsh Arabs, who lived in the region.

- The regime carried out mass executions of dissidents during the March 1991 uprising in the cities of southern Iraq.[5]

- The regime occasionally carries out mass executions of prisoners, especially those who have been sentenced to long terms.[6]

Toward a More Hopeful Future

Throughout more than three decades of terror, the people of Iraq have survived on hope. This hope has united almost all Iraqi opposition factions, along with the majority of the Iraqi people, in the desire to remake post-Saddam Iraq into a civil society, with a democratic, pluralistic, law-respecting, federalist system of government that ensures self-determination, human rights, and the principles of justice. Such a transformation will not be easy. First, a future Iraq cannot be envisaged without strong outside military support; any suggestion of change from within is sheer hypocrisy. Certain measures must also be taken in advance to avert bloodshed, chaos, and looting following any such military action.

Second, since taking power, the Ba'ath regime has reconstituted Iraq's executive, judiciary, and legislative branches—along with its political, social, educational, and cultural institutions—to serve the political purposes, and even the personal wishes, of its totalitarian leadership. Hence, every aspect of official life in a post-Saddam Iraq would need to be changed, from the presidency down to the lowest levels of authority. Fundamental amendments to the structures, laws, and internal regulations of virtually every Iraqi institution would be required, along with a near total replacement of the decisionmaking bureaucracy.

The first step in reaching these goals would be reconstruction of the legal system. A team of lawmakers, lawyers, human rights activists, and politicians representing all ethnic, religious, sectarian, and ideological classes in Iraqi society should draft a constitution guaranteeing democracy, freedom, human rights, and a checks-and-balances system of governance. The constitution must be based on a federal system, widely considered to be the most suitable framework for multinational states. The Iraqi Kurdistan Regional Parliament—elected on May 19, 1992, in a democratic process unprecedented in many neighboring countries—has already unanimously adopted the federal system in defining its legal relation to the central government; hence, a post-Saddam Iraq would be unable to achieve peace and stability if it sought a nondemocratic solution to the Kurdish question.

Soon after a change in government took place, a national conference would need to be held outside of Iraq in order to legalize the actions taken to change the regime, assume full responsibility for the consequences of these actions, widen the base of decisionmaking, narrow the differences between various Iraqi groups, and pave the way for a stable Iraq. In addition, such a conference should take the following concrete actions: ratify the proposed constitution; nominate a head of state or a supreme council; appoint an interim gov-

ernment; select a legislative or consultative council; and declare an amnesty (as discussed in detail in the next section).
The conferees should be made up of representatives from all
political parties and opposition groups as well as human rights
activists and experts in administration, law, economics, industry, agriculture, diplomacy, education, social affairs, the
military, the environment, and so forth.

Once reforms were completed, and before the post-Saddam transitional stage (which should be kept to a minimum)
expired, general elections would need to be held throughout Iraq. A democratically elected assembly of representatives
and a president should be installed in each region. Likewise,
provision should be made for the election of a federal parliament (a house of representatives and a house of regions) and
a federal president whose first duties would be to adopt, ratify,
and legalize all pending constitutions, laws, and government
initiatives.

The enactment of the constitution could be delayed, of
course, until the transitional period expired, at which time it
could be ratified by an elected, constituent-based assembly.
The constitution must be ratified by both the regional and
central parliaments, or by the people themselves in a general
referendum. The danger in such an approach is that the current balance between Iraqi opposition groups may change in
such a manner that one particular faction assumes sufficient
power to demand special privileges for itself or to deny others their rights. In any case, all of these measures would signal
the beginning of a process leading toward a peaceful, democratic, and prosperous Iraq.

Holding Senior Officials Accountable

True reconciliation could not begin, however, until the senior members of Saddam's regime were called to account for
their crimes. If this were not done in an official manner, victims and/or their families could take matters into their own
hands, thereby creating a new cycle of violence in post-Saddam Iraq. The despicable crimes perpetrated under Saddam
must be publicly acknowledged and discussed, not swept un-

der the carpet; exposing these crimes to both the Iraqi people and the outside world would be the only means of preventing unsanctioned retribution and ensuring that such crimes were never committed again.

In its very first public statement, the first post-Saddam administration should reassure Iraqi citizens that it is not simply another link in the chain of coups and so-called revolutions that have plagued modern Iraq. It should stress that a new era has begun, an era in which every individual has both a right and a duty to participate in creating a civil society and a tolerant, democratic, pluralistic, law-abiding political system that governs through constitutional institutions legitimately elected by the people. Nevertheless, the old regime's crimes should be dealt with during the inevitable transitional period: the crimes must be disclosed, the fate of the victims must be revealed, an official apology must be made, and the perpetrators must be brought to trial. The patience and support of the people would be essential during this period.

The crimes of Saddam's regime have not been sporadic, random events in which irresponsible officials acted on their own. These crimes were, and still are, conducted according to premeditated policies, with the full sanction of the highest levels of authority. Identifying the perpetrators is therefore not a difficult task, for they are the same officials who have issued orders for the planning of criminal actions; participated in subsequent preparations for these actions; and, in the case of certain high-ranking individuals, ordered the implementation of the plans. Besides Saddam himself, the institutions responsible for these crimes are the Revolutionary Command Council, the Ba'ath Party Regional Command, the Council of Ministers, the Armed Forces General Staff, the Republican Guard Corps General Staff, the National Security Council, the Emergency Forces General Staff, the Popular Army General Staff, the Intelligence Directorate, the Special Security Directorate, the General Security Directorate, and the Revolutionary Courts.

National reconciliation can be achieved only through the trial and punishment of the main perpetrators within

Saddam's regime and through a declaration of amnesty for so-called junior perpetrators. Following Saddam's removal, indictments could be issued by a special prosecutor, but only after an impartial, just, and legal investigation in which UN standards were observed. At the same time, individual victims must be given the right to request that this prosecutor take action against those whom they accuse of committing crimes against them.

The Legal Process

The first article of the Iraqi Code of Criminal Procedure[7] states the following: "No punishment for an act, except according to a law incriminating it at the time of its perpetration." It has been proven beyond doubt that this code has been violated; that horrible crimes have been committed by the regime; that numerous national, international, and humanitarian laws have been breached (see box, next page); and that the perpetrators of many of these crimes can be identified by name for indictment. Aside from the overwhelming evidence that would be readily available following the overthrow of the current regime (e.g., the large number of eyewitnesses and the numerous official documents that would surely be confiscated), thousands of incriminating official documents were captured during the 1991 uprising and transferred to the United States for classification. As one commentator put it, "For the first time in history, a regime's damning human-rights record was exposed by its own documents while it was still in power."[8]

To ensure that the trials of accused persons are conducted within a legal framework, an ad hoc tribunal should be established, a special prosecutor appointed, and a special law enacted. Such procedures are not unprecedented in Iraq's history. The most famous example may be the court-martial of the prominent members of the monarchy after the so-called revolution of July 14, 1958. At that time, the special "Law for the Punishment of the Conspirators on the Safety of the Homeland and the Corruption of the Ruling System" was enacted.

Laws Governing Crimes Committed by Saddam's Regime

- The 1925 Geneva Protocol for the Prohibition of the Use in War of Asphyxiating, Poisonous, or Other Gases, and of Bacteriological Methods of Warfare
- United Nations Charter, 1945
- Convention on the Prevention and Punishment of the Crime of Genocide, United Nations, 1948
- Universal Declaration of Human Rights, 1948
- Geneva Conventions, 1949
- International Convention on the Elimination of All Forms of Racial Discrimination, United Nations, 1965
- International Covenant on Civil and Political Rights, United Nations, 1966
- International Covenant on Economical, Social, and Cultural Rights, United Nations, 1966
- Declaration on the Elimination of Discrimination against Women, United Nations, 1967
- International Convention on the Suppression and Punishment of the Crime of Apartheid, United Nations, 1973
- Declaration on the Protection of All Persons from Being Subjected to Torture and Other Cruel, Inhuman, or Degrading Treatment or Punishment, United Nations, 1975
- Code of Conduct for Law Enforcement Officials, United Nations, 1979
- Declaration on the Elimination of All Forms of Intolerance and of Discrimination Based on Religion or Belief, United Nations, 1981
- Safeguards Guaranteeing Protection of the Rights of Those Facing the Death Penalty, 1984
- Declaration on the Right of Peoples to Peace, United Nations, 1984
- United Nations Standard Minimum Rules for the Administration of Juvenile Justice, 1985
- Principles on the Effective Prevention and Investigation of Extra-legal, Arbitrary, and Summary Executions, United Nations, 1989
- Basic Principles on the Use of Force and Firearms by Law Enforcement Officials, United Nations, 1990
- Declaration on the Protection of All Persons from Enforced Disappearance, United Nations, 1992
- United Nations Security Council Resolution 688 (regarding repression of Iraqi civilians), 1991

A post-Saddam tribunal could also be empowered with jurisdiction over those Iraqis who have committed international crimes, providing a unique precedent in bringing war criminals to justice in front of a national court in their native country. After all, the wars waged by Saddam's regime against neighboring states have had devastating internal as well as external consequences, including a half-million Iraqi casualties, the destruction of Iraq's infrastructure, UN sanctions, and the labeling of the country as a warmonger.

Post-Saddam criminal proceedings could follow the example of various international precedents, including the Nuremberg and Japanese war-criminal proceedings and, more recently, the war-criminal trials in the former Yugoslavia. Reconciliation precedents can also be found in the South African and German reunification models. Unprecedented, however, is the extent of the atrocities that the current Iraqi regime has inflicted on its own people. No ethnic, religious, sectarian, or political group has been spared—not even members of the ruling party itself. Most every Iraqi citizen has either lost a relative or friend or been personally subjected to inhuman or degrading treatment. From the perspective of the victims and their families, indicting a mere two or three dozen persons as the sole perpetrators of these crimes would be insufficient.

In the prosecution of any crime, it is a principle of justice to limit the time period of the conspiracy (to borrow terminology used in the Nuremberg trials) by establishing an agreed-upon starting point. The consensus among Iraqis is that 1979, when Saddam took power, is an appropriate landmark year. Consequently, the scope of a post-Saddam investigation should include those individuals who were in charge of the relevant offices from that time onward.

Finally, after indicting suspects, a special prosecutor would probably demand capital punishment for some (since the death penalty is in force in the Iraqi Code of Criminal Procedure) and long- or short-term prison sentences for others, according to the gravity of their crimes.

Amnesty

The largest group of Iraqi criminal perpetrators can be found among the 400,000 servicemen in the security forces. Using legal procedures to hold all of these men accountable for the crimes they have committed would be impractical. Such measures may even be unjust, given that the vast majority of these individuals carried out crimes under the strict orders and watchful eyes of their superiors, who have been known to execute servicemen for disobedience.

In order to ensure justice and dissuade the security forces from fighting for Saddam as a means of protecting themselves, a declaration of amnesty would be an essential part of any plans for regime change. During the Gulf War, in anticipation of some form of uprising inside Iraq, the Kurdistan Front (an alliance of Kurdish political parties) declared an amnesty for the previously mentioned Kurdish *jash* forces on the Iraqi army payroll. By this astute act, the Kurdistan Front succeeded in persuading the *jash* to switch sides and support the uprising, which allowed the Kurds to gain control of Iraqi Kurdistan fairly quickly. Declaring this sort of amnesty in a post-Saddam Iraq could minimize casualties in the short term, even while promising justice in the long term.

Naturally, any amnesty should explicitly exclude the senior members of the regime who have committed crimes against the Iraqi people or the citizens of other countries. In addition, it should not protect the perpetrators of certain types of crimes that are inexcusable no matter what the perpetrator's rank. It should be stressed that an amnesty would cover only criminal prosecutions and that special civil measures should be taken against lesser perpetrators.

The question of loyalists must also be addressed as part of the post-Saddam accountability and amnesty process. For more than three decades, Saddam's regime, while busily eliminating the supposed enemies of the state, worked to create a class of supporters consisting of Ba'ath Party members, security agents, so-called public organizations (of youths, women, laborers, etc.), propagandists, mercenaries, and collaborators. In return for their aid in carrying out the criminal policies of the regime, these people enjoyed special privileges while the rest of the Iraqi populace suffered from starvation and oppression.

What role would this class play in post-Saddam Iraq? Would they form a fifth column and attempt to regain the power, influence, and privileges they once enjoyed? Clearly, special measures must be employed to obviate this possibility. Two international precedents offer examples of such measures. First, following the overthrow of the Egyptian monarchy in 1952, the classes that had supported the old regime (mostly wealthy landowners and capitalists) were deprived of potential resources for destabilizing the new regime. Their property was subjected to sequestration, and limitations were placed on their civil rights. Second, in postunification Germany, former agents of East Germany were denied government employment while victims of the East German regime were given the right to read their secret files (with the names of the informers removed) and to prosecute the perpetrators of crimes against them.

Interim Steps

Finally, measures must be taken even before the fall of Saddam's regime to ensure that its crimes are not repeated by any future regime. A pan-Iraqi human rights organization consisting exclusively of independent and impartial volunteer members should be established as soon as possible in order to monitor the human rights situation in Iraq, particularly following Saddam's ouster. This organization should have a clear mandate to publicly report human rights violations committed by post-Saddam authorities, so that the horrors of his regime do not once again become the status quo.

Notes

1. United Nations General Assembly Resolution 260 (December 9, 1948), Article 2. Available online (www.unhchr.ch/html/menu3/b/ p_genoci.htm).

2. For a detailed account of this campaign, as well as of the Halabja chemical attack described in subsequent paragraphs, see *Genocide in*

Iraq: The Anfal Campaign against the Kurds (New York: Human Rights Watch, July 1993). Available online (www.hrw.org/reports/1993/iraqanfal/).

3. Helena Cook, *The Safe Haven in Northern Iraq: International Responsibility for Iraqi Kurdistan* (London: Human Rights Center/Kurdish Human Rights Project, 1995).

4. Ibid.

5. Ibid.

6. Confidential reports obtained from Iraqi Communist Party members inside Iraq.

7. The basic elements of the code have been in force since they were first issued in 1918 by the supreme commander of the British occupation forces in Iraq. Its modern equivalent was first institutionalized as Law No. 23 of 1971, published in Iraq's *Official Gazette*.

8. Jonathan Randal, *After Such Knowledge, What Forgiveness?* (Boulder, Colo.: Westview Press, 1998), p. 255.

Amatzia Baram

Viewing Regime Change through a Historical Lens

Iraq's history, social makeup, and political culture would play a significant role in determining what sort of state emerged following the fall of Saddam Husayn's regime. In particular, years of anti-Western propaganda would likely complicate relations with the West, while a long tradition of internal divisiveness and violence could make it difficult to ensure stability. This essay examines the fundamental elements of that tradition and analyzes some of the key challenges that could emerge in a post-Saddam Iraq, such as countering threats to U.S. forces in the immediate aftermath of Saddam's removal; balancing tribal autonomy and national unity; maintaining the military's important social role while purging its ranks of criminal and loyalist elements; retraining the Iraqi educated class; assimilating returning émigrés; resuscitating the economy; and dealing with other countries in the region that may or may not look favorably on a new regime in Baghdad.

The Historical Legacy

The modern state of Iraq was born in 1920 from the union of three disparate Ottoman provinces; because the British colonial power served as midwife, the newborn state was shaped almost entirely according to imperial interests. This circumstance exacerbated the problems that confronted the first regime in Baghdad. The already sharp ethnic, denominational, and regional fault lines between and among Shi'i Arabs, Sunni Arabs, and Sunni Kurds were widened in light of the fact that power was, and still is, largely in the hands of the

69

Sunni Arab minority, which has long constituted only 15 to 20 percent of the population.

Under the monarchy (1921–1958), much of this Sunni minority was willing to share a measure of the country's wealth with the Shi'i and Kurdish tribal and landed elite. In reality, however, the monopoly on power and wealth was limited to a tiny group that enriched itself through officially endorsed corruption of monstrous proportions. This wealth came at the expense of a largely pauperized citizenry, including the destitute Shi'is in the sprawling shantytowns of northeast Baghdad and the impoverished, powerless, yet wildly nationalistic Effendiya (the Western-educated, mainly Sunni Arab lower-middle class) in large towns throughout the country.

Given this context, neither the Iraqi monarchy nor the subsequent military and Ba'ath regimes enjoyed any meaningful degree of legitimacy at the grassroots level. A combination of various factors—corruption, socioeconomic exploitation, minority rule, sharp ideological divisions, factionalism, and the lack of any mechanisms for reasonable power-sharing—was sufficient to create alienation and resentment among much of the general public. Even the Sunni ruling minority itself has long been divided by regional and tribal rivalries.

Such problems have sparked numerous revolts, whether due to intertribal disagreements, pan-Arab and anti-British sentiments, ethnic and denominational antipathy, or socioeconomic friction between peasants and landlords. Between 1919 and 1958, Iraq suffered eight Kurdish revolts, nine Shi'i revolts, four major city riots, three coups d'état, one anti-Assyrian pogrom, and two anti-Jewish pogroms.

Beginning with Sati' al-Husri, the monarchy's first director of education, and continuing decades later under Saddam Husayn, the Iraqi ruling elite usually sought to contain such unrest and attain legitimacy by resorting to rhetoric (and, occasionally, policies) that were jingoistic and fiercely pan-Arab. For example, it was Iraq, more than any other Arab state, that pushed the Arab League to invade Palestine on May 15, 1948; Iraqi regent 'Abd al-Illah did so partly in order to suppress ominous public demonstrations in his own country. Similarly, although the regime's decision to refrain from action in Jordan during Black September 1970 saved Iraq from disaster, Iraqi leaders sent a huge force to the Golan Heights in 1973 for fear that further inaction would be unacceptable to the Iraqi public. Nowhere more than in Iraq has the saying "Patriotism is the refuge of the scoundrel" held true. Even disgruntled Iraqi Shi'is were less volatile when the country was actively fighting the "Zionist entity."

The only two exceptions to this trend were the first three years of General Abd al-Karim Qasim's rule (which began in 1958) and the period between 1974 and 1980. In both cases, major investments in the economy and significant social improvements won a measure of legitimacy for the regimes and enabled them to lower their anti-Israel profile. Yet, both regimes eventually lost this legitimacy; Qasim suffered setbacks in his military offensive against the Kurds and did not have sufficient resources to continue his reforms, while the Ba'ath regime, under Saddam, launched its ill-fated war against Iran.

Today, the central government in Iraq is far stronger in relation to other components of Iraqi society than it has been at any time in history. Nevertheless, intertribal conflicts still erupt periodically, in addition to occasional skirmishes between tribes and Saddam's regime. Because it has far fewer resources to distribute than it did during the late 1970s and 1980s, the regime resorts to more violence and repression. Despite these repressive powers, the regime still feels that it needs to prove its pan-Arab, anti-Israeli, and anti-Western credentials in order to win legitimacy from Iraq's vast lower-middle class (including the army and Republican Guard officer corps), whether or not this strategy actually works.

Shi'i Unrest

Although some of the historical causes for Shi'i peasant revolts have dissipated over time (e.g., following the land reforms enacted under General Qasim and the Ba'ath), other factors have continued to spark occasional eruptions, making Shi'i discontent even more acute. First, secular Shi'is have, at best, been only partially integrated into the ruling elite during any given period. Even when, during the early 1970s, Shi'i Ba'ath activists began to surface in senior government, military, and party positions, real power remained in Sunni Arab hands. Shi'is could rise through the Ba'ath Party quickly, but only up to a certain point, beyond which they were not represented in meaningful proportions. Shi'is constituted nearly 70 percent of the party's membership, but many felt that low- and mid-level Shi'i officials were simply managing the party for their Sunni masters.

Second, the Shi'i religious establishment and its many traditional followers resented the secular policies of General Qasim and the subsequent Ba'ath regime. Under Qasim, however, this resentment was counterbalanced by extensive socioeconomic improvements. Qasim encouraged Shi'is to rise to senior positions in the army and government. He also distributed land to peasants and initiated a vast housing program for the numerous Shi'i shantytown dwellers of Baghdad. Although Qasim abolished the tribal regulations that gave shaykhs dictatorial power over their tribesmen—a practice that permanently alienated certain tribes from the Iraqi government—he was careful not to declare war on those shaykhs whom the tribes needed as leaders and arbiters. Perhaps most important, Qasim carefully refrained from interfering with traditional Shi'i autonomy, represented mainly by autonomous religious institutions such as the Circles of Learning (religious universities). Colonel Abd al-Salam Arif, who collaborated with the Ba'ath to overthrow Qasim in 1963, adopted a similar strategy.

Yet, the subsequent Ba'ath regime of Maj. Gen. Ahmad Hasan al-Bakr—under the guiding hand of Saddam Husayn, the czar of internal security—strayed from this policy in June 1969, when it decided to nationalize the Shi'i educational and religious system. The result was a major confrontation between the more traditional segments of the Shi'i population and the government. Even many less traditional Shi'is were offended by the intrusive Ba'ath policies. Similar confrontations occurred on a smaller scale in 1977 and 1979, along with a more widespread Shi'i revolt in March 1991.

Regime-Shi'i tension in Iraq has grown even more acute over the last two decades, in part because of the regime's neglect of Shi'i infrastructure in the southern part of the country. To begin with, the most destructive battles of the Iran-Iraq War were waged in southern Iraq, causing maximal damage to Shi'i areas. Further damage was caused by the Gulf War, the 1991 Shi'i uprising, and the international sanctions on Iraq. Since then, the government has done relatively little to repair the infrastructure in these areas, in an apparent attempt to punish the Shi'is for their uprising. As a result, water purification and sewage systems are largely inoperative in southern Iraq, causing high rates of disease and child mortality. Moreover, hospitals in the south have been neglected, and food rations have been cut off at times in areas that exhibit open opposition to the government.

In order to deflect the resultant Shi'i anger, Saddam has often resorted to the mainstay of past Iraqi regimes: anti-Jewish and anti-Western (in Saddam's case, anti-American) incitement. Assessing the overall success of this virulent propaganda is impossible; judging by personal interviews with Shi'i activists who fled Iraq in 1991, however, the anti-Jewish incitement has had a significant impact.

Finally, since 1969, between 250,000 and 400,000 Iraqi Shi'is have fled (or been driven) to Iran as a result of confrontations with the Ba'ath regime. Several thousand of these refugees have joined the Badr Brigade of the Supreme Assembly of the Islamic Revolution in Iraq (SAIRI), an Iraqi opposition group originally formed, and still based, in Iran. The opposition group al-Da'wa al-Islamiyya (Islamic call) has gained support in Iran as well, and both groups have underground affiliates inside Iraq. Currently, these groups are too weak for a full-scale uprising, but if Saddam were forced to deal with an American invasion, they could spark a Shi'i revolution and attempt to influence Iraq's post-Saddam future from a fairly strong position.

Political Violence and Repression

The Iraqi central government's historical reliance on violence—whether directed at Kurds, Shi'is, or other potential sources of opposition—would itself have a significant impact on any post-Saddam scenario. Iraqi revolts have been more numerous and more violent than those in other Middle Eastern countries, and the responses of Iraqi regimes have always been harsher. This trend of violent revolts and violent repression reached an unprecedented level under the Ba'ath regime, largely due to Saddam Husayn's influence. For example, approximately 100,000 Iraqi Kurds were killed when the government crushed several revolts between 1975 and 1988. Similarly, between 30,000 and 60,000 Shi'is were killed during their major revolt in southern Iraq in March 1991.

Violence has also characterized the Iraqi political system since its inception. Iraq was the first Arab country to experience a successful military coup d'etat (the Bakr-Sidqi coup in 1936). Military officers dominated Iraqi political life for several years thereafter, resulting in a great deal of political havoc and violence. Later, in 1952, the monarchy involved military forces in political repression in Baghdad for the first time when it was unable to put an end to massive riots through other means; previously, the military had only been used to crush Kurdish and Shi'i revolts in other parts of the country.

This empowerment of the military proved disastrous. In 1958, army officers led by Qasim destroyed the monarchy, whereupon several military juntas ruled Iraq in violent succession until 1970. With few exceptions, their rule was typified by political unrest, economic chaos, animosity toward neighboring countries, and military adventurism. On the whole, these regimes failed at both domestic governance and foreign relations, despite receiving massive Soviet support. For the most part, none of Iraq's military regimes have enjoyed significant legitimacy among the general population; even many Sunni Arabs have regarded them as illegitimate.

As a result of this legacy, Saddam's regime introduced a vast surveillance system to keep the population in check, in the form of hundreds of thousands of spies—some paid, some unpaid, some voluntary, some involuntary. Today, the Iraqi population is largely policing itself, much like the East Germans did during the Soviet era. In general, Iraqis are very careful in their relations with their fellow citizens, aside from close family members and friends; any one of them could be Saddam's willing or reluctant agent provocateur.

It is anyone's guess how thirty years of property confiscation, torture, executions, fear, hate, and deep suspicion have affected social relations in Iraq. One can safely assume, however, that, if the heavy sealing lid of violent repression were lifted following Saddam's ouster, the temptation to settle accounts would be great. The remainder of this essay will explore potentially volatile areas of Iraqi society and suggest ways to minimize the danger of a breakdown of public order under a post-Saddam regime.

Immediate Aftermath of Saddam's Removal

Following Saddam's removal, many Iraqis may succumb to a sense of anarchical freedom, given the conditions under which they have lived for several decades. Violence could erupt in several different forms, including intertribal bloodshed, Shi'i-led anti-Sunni riots, class riots in Baghdad (where socioeconomic inequality is glaring), and revenge attacks against Iraqi Intelligence Service and Ba'ath apparatchiks who tortured citizens under Saddam's rule. Moreover, the dismissal of many former security personnel could increase violent crime and lead to widespread mafia-style activity. All of these scenarios would pose major threats to the stability and legitimacy of a new regime. Therefore, the Iraqi military would likely have to supplement aggressive police work in order to curtail such crime; given Iraq's history, this would not be an ideal role for the military, but it could prove necessary following Saddam's removal.

If regime change were achieved through a major U.S. military campaign, U.S. troops would have to remain in Iraq for some time. Even if they were embraced by a largely grateful Iraqi population (which is a likely scenario), the fact remains that U.S. soldiers would represent an ideal target for underground Ba'ath cells, al-Qaeda terrorists, Shi'i fundamentalists (e.g., from al-Da'wa al-Islamiyya), or even criminals hoping to loot weapons. Therefore, the United States would likely find itself between the horns of a dilemma. If it evacuated its military forces soon after toppling Saddam, it would be unable to ensure the new regime's stability. If U.S. troops remained in major Iraqi cities, however, they would be in harm's way.

The solution may be to establish an international force that could take over immediately following the withdrawal of American troops. If such a solution proved unworkable, American forces would have to establish their bases in the empty desert areas of western Iraq, far enough to distance themselves from potential attackers, but close enough to intervene quickly in the event of an assault on the new regime. Basing U.S. troops in Saddam's large and well-fortified palace compounds in Baghdad would be a mistake; such a move would be perceived by the Iraqi public as a signal that foreign forces were simply taking the place of Saddam. Instead, Saddam's palaces and compounds must be placed at the public's disposal immediately after his removal. They could serve as college campuses, as holiday resorts for Iraqi soldiers, as recreation and recuperation centers for underprivileged or malnourished children, or most any other role, as long as they were open to the public.

U.S. troops could stay in the al-Rashid military camp in Baghdad temporarily, but they would need to leave the capital as soon as possible. In their place, a reliable Iraqi army unit could assume control over al-Rashid and work to prevent any potential Ba'ath resurgence or military coup. As long as U.S. forces were in Baghdad, however, they would need to be fully reinforced, with artillery, heavy armor, and helicopter gunships available at a moment's notice. Moreover, furloughs in Baghdad would need to be kept to a minimum so that U.S. troops were not unduly exposed to potential attacks. Given the U.S. experience in Somalia, the Iraqi Ba'ath remnants would likely pin their hopes on a lack of U.S. staying power; therefore, the United States could not afford to show any signs of weak resolve.

Managing Tribal Relations after Saddam

Under Saddam Husayn, many Sunni, Shi'i, and Kurdish tribal shaykhs have been given weapons, land, money, and great authority over their tribes, which has greatly increased their autonomy from the state. In exchange, these tribes have monitored Iraq's borders to guard against infiltration and to prevent their own tribesmen from joining the anti-Ba'ath guerrilla fighters. Given this autonomy, tribal law and practices (*'urf, 'adah*) have prevailed in the Iraqi countryside for quite some time, often taking precedence over national law. For example, the regime has tolerated tribal practices such as blood feud and peacemaking (*sulha*), compensatory blood money (*diyyeh*), and the murder of women to protect family honor (*'ird*). Indeed, men who are guilty of the latter offense are often acquitted in the state courts, assuming they are even turned in to state authorities in the first place.

In light of these conditions, a post-Saddam regime should interfere as little as possible in intra- and intertribal affairs, at least initially. At the same time, a new regime would need to emphasize that tribes are not completely autonomous from the state, clearly delineating those matters of law and governance in which state control is in effect. This was, more or less, the policy adopted by Saddam, and there would be no need for radical change immediately following his removal; in general, a new regime should handle the tribes with a combination of money, diplomacy, and force.

In the countryside, tribal shaykhs could be a useful financial conduit, receiving resources from Baghdad and disseminating them to their tribesmen. A new government would need to monitor these resources, however, ensuring that the shaykhs' allocations were reasonably equitable. If certain groups within a tribe complained that a shaykh was discriminating against them, the government would have a powerful countermeasure: it could allow these groups to become independent and nominate their own shaykhs. This would represent a blow to the old shaykh and serve as an example to others. At the same time, it would guarantee loyalty on the part of the newly independent groups.

Similarly, a new government could punish unjust shaykhs by allowing their constituents to hold democratic elections for a new local authority (e.g., a mayor). If the government lent its support to such new leaders, both they and their constituents would become loyal to the state, all at the expense of the old shaykh. Yet, any potential new authority would need to gain significant local popularity before supplanting the old shaykh.

Depending on the wishes of the people, a new regime could also allow shaykhs to represent their constituents at the capital, while providing an alternative avenue by which individuals could reach government officials. In addition, any post-Saddam regime would need to avoid the discriminatory policies of the past on contentious issues involving different sectors of Iraqi society and government (e.g., water distribution). Although a new regime may be tempted to show favoritism in deciding such issues, it would be better served by implementing equitable policies based on the recommendations of knowledgeable government officials. Tribes would be more likely to accede to Baghdad's wishes if they regarded the central government as essentially just.

In the event of serious tribal crime, a new regime would need to intervene immediately, particularly in cases of murder or grievous injury. This does not mean that the government should impose its procedures and decisions in all cases; rather, a traditional mechanism should be established to help resolve such problems. For example, in the event of an intertribal murder, the government should immediately arrest the murderer pending state trial. In the meantime, it should help the tribes in question establish a *majlis shuyukh* (Shaykh's council) to serve as an arbiter. The men chosen to serve on this majlis must be well known and highly respected. In addition, the very fact that the government was placing its seal on the majlis would enhance the personal prestige of these men, lending greater weight to the majlis itself and creating new bonds between the government and the majlis members. Moreover, if the majlis resolved the problem through traditional measures (e.g., *diyyeh*), the state court could lighten its own sentence. In any event, a new government would need to involve itself in some fashion; otherwise, intertribal relations would quickly become chaotic.

Regarding weapons, the tribes must be disarmed to a certain extent. Tribal Iraqis have had rifles for hundreds of years and would not surrender them to any regime. Nevertheless, a post-Saddam regime would need to confiscate more powerful weapons immediately, including heavy machine guns, mortars, and armored cars, all of which are prevalent throughout the tribal regions. The tribes should be required to give up their military capabilities and, to a large extent, their political power in exchange for economic benefits. Achieving this goal while minimizing crime and chaos in the tribal hinterland would require a major campaign to establish social and economic services in these regions, similar to the Ba'ath regime's improvement efforts throughout the 1970s.

Finally, those tribes that have been collaborating with the Ba'ath regime since 1968 might have difficulty working with a new government. Therefore, a post-Saddam regime may need to employ special measures to ensure the cooperation of these tribes. Toward this end, such tribes should be identified before potential difficulties arise. For example, the Shi'i branch of Saddam's own tribe, the Albu Nasir, has long collaborated with his regime, particularly the group led by Husayn Sayyid 'Ali, residing in and around Najaf. At the same time, however, other branches of this tribe have become somewhat alienated from Saddam over the years due to his harsh disciplinary actions. Moreover, certain branches of other tribes are implicitly (though not actively) opposed to Saddam's regime (e.g., members of the Dulaym, 'Ubayd, Jubbur, and Shaya'isha tribes, and many residents of Samarra).

Increasing Shi'i Representation

Historically, Iraqi Shi'is have been less volatile during periods when the vast majority of them could identify, more or less, with their government leaders. The Shi'i community is

heterogeneous; although many Shi'is are still rather traditional, others are quite secular. As a result, the struggle for
power and influence among senior Shi'i clergy in Iraq is currently as contentious as that seen in Iran. Therefore, if a new
Iraqi regime hoped to create a representative government
that was acceptable to the majority of Shi'is, it would need to
ensure that various rival camps were represented, including
secular factions. A new regime must also ensure that those
camps supported by Iranian radicals do not monopolize
power; these groups would never surrender such a monopoly,
and any hope of democratization would therefore be lost.

During the March 1991 Shi'i uprising, only one leader
was accepted by all of the revolutionaries throughout the Shi'i
south: Grand Ayat Allah Abu al-Qasim al-Kho'i. This is particularly significant in light of the fact that Kho'i was an Azeri,
not an Arab, and that he opposed the notion of a political
clergy (i.e., Ayatollah Ruhollah Khomeini's formula of the
"rule of the religious jurist," as implemented in Iran). Although Iraq currently has few such unifying clergymen, many
highly respected Iraqi figures are living in Europe—beyond
the reach of both the Iranian mullahs and Saddam—and
could therefore make good candidates for representation in
a new Iraqi government.

One such figure is Hujjat al-Islam wal-Muslimin
Muhammad Bahr al-'Ulum, who manages the London-based
Center of Ahl al-Bayt. Similarly, Abd al-Majid Kho'i, the elder
son of Abu al-Qasim al-Kho'i, is well known and well liked in
the Iraqi Shi'i community, although he resides in London
and is not a clergyman in his own right. His views, which he
makes public in both English and Arabic, are moderate and
anti-Ba'ath. Much like his father, he is not a fan of the Iranian radicals.

In addition to political representation, Shi'is must be
granted equal opportunity to participate in other sectors of
the Iraqi state. In particular, the military and security apparatuses must become more inclusive. Shi'i city dwellers have
suffered the most government discrimination of all, largely
due to the Ba'ath perception that rural, tribal Shi'is are true

Arabs, while urban Shi'is are susceptible to Persian cultural influences and therefore potentially treasonous.

Although inclusion of Shi'is would be crucial, any new Iraqi government must remain mindful of the danger that Shi'i fundamentalist control over southern Iraq would pose. Of all the Iraqi fundamentalist opposition groups, the only ones that currently have some degree of organization inside Iraq proper are the Shi'i groups SAIRI and al-Da'wa al-Islamiyya. These groups would almost certainly try to establish control in the south following Saddam's removal, and they must be prevented from doing so at all costs. A new regime must establish adequate security before permitting such groups to participate in the process of democratization.

Moreover, a post-Saddam government would need to focus its development efforts on the Shi'i south in order to quell deep public resentment. As described previously, the entire region—particularly the 'Amara district—is currently suffering from the Ba'ath regime's longstanding neglect, with severe child malnutrition among the most visible consequences. If a post-Saddam regime did not give priority to these problems, it would face widespread public protest that could be exploited by Iran and by Shi'i fundamentalists in Iraq. A new regime must avoid the temptation to adopt Saddam's approach to development, namely, prioritizing Baghdad above all other areas in order to avoid riots in the capital.

Assessing Kurdish Autonomy

Between 1919 and 1991 (with a long lull between 1945 and 1961), the Kurdish zones of Iraq were in a near constant state of revolt. Although various Kurdish tribes and groups cooperated with certain Iraqi regimes, many others fought against these regimes and were consequently subjected to horrendous repression. After the Kurds won autonomous status in 1991, they instituted a measure of democratic rule and experienced relative economic prosperity.

Given this context, Iraqi Kurds would not accept any post-Saddam arrangement that stripped them of the benefits they have gained under autonomy. In fact, they would likely demand a significant share of power in any new central government. Maintaining some degree of Kurdish autonomy without undermining Iraqi national unity would require extensive, tense negotiations. However it was defined, autonomy of some sort would be necessary in order to secure existing Kurdish achievements, provide an outlet for Kurdish national sentiments, and put an end to Kurdish revolts.

The most difficult issue in the Kurdish arena has long been the fate of the Kirkuk oil fields in northern Iraq. Recently, both the Kurds and the Iraqi Turkomans have demanded control over Kirkuk, but there is no support for these demands among Arab political circles in Iraq and abroad. If, under a new regime, the Kurds were satisfied that their share of Iraqi national resources was fair, the Kirkuk controversy would be greatly diffused.

Restructuring the Military and Internal Security Apparatuses

Despite its defeats in most military engagements, its role in crushing the March 1991 uprisings, and its mediocre performance during the Iran-Iraq War, the Iraqi military is still a respected symbol of Iraqi nationalism in the eyes of the Iraqi public. Therefore, it could become an indispensable tool for returning Iraq to normalcy following Saddam's removal. Before it could assume this role, however, it would need to be purged of overtly political officers and Ba'ath political institutions (e.g., the Political Guidance Department).

Fortunately, Saddam has carefully distanced the military from any policymaking role—a positive legacy that should prove helpful under a new, civilian regime. At the same time, however, Iraqi military officers have long been forced to join the Ba'ath Party and participate in indoctrination sessions. After thirty years of such indoctrination, they would need some degree of deprogramming under a new regime, including lessons on the role of the armed forces in democratic governments. Moreover, the various regional, tribal, and denominational alliances and hegemonies within the officer corps would need to be dissolved; this would help to open up a large reservoir of military talent.

The most important military-related task of a new regime would be to dismantle the Republican and Special Republican Guard corps. Officers in these units are highly politicized; they are initially chosen for their loyalty and then pampered by the president in order to maintain this loyalty. Therefore, few of them would be fit for service under a new regime. The more apolitical Republican Guard officers could be integrated into the regular army, as long as they were dispersed among different units. Similarly, the Presidential Protection (Himayat al-Ra'is, or al-Himaya) as a whole would have to be disbanded. The few thousand members of this commando unit are in charge of Saddam's security and have a deep personal loyalty to him. The new regime must pay special attention to the various paramilitary units, particularly Saddam's Fida'iyyin (Martyrs), presently under the command of his elder son 'Udayy. This militia has committed countless atrocities since its creation in 1995, so every soldier and officer in its ranks must be pensioned off without exception.

Post-Saddam Iraq would still need a reasonably strong army for its national defense. The regular army should consist of between 250,000 and 300,000 troops. In addition, it would need new weapons, including a few hundred new tanks and combat aircraft. The United States may want to supply these weapons, if only to ensure that they are carefully calibrated to serve defensive purposes.

It is unclear what stance Iraqi military officers would assume regarding the role of weapons of mass destruction (WMD) and medium- and long-range missiles in a post-Saddam era. When Saddam decided to embark on a nuclear weapons program, he apparently did not consult with his senior military officers, so their attitude toward such programs is unknown. In any case, a post-Saddam regime would need to emphasize to military leaders that no additional WMD will be developed and that existing WMD must be destroyed. If a new regime attempted to gain popularity with the officer corps by promising to turn Iraq into a nonconventional power, the United States would need to intervene immediately. The Iraqi officer corps must accept the notion that their country's vast resources are sufficient to ensure homeland defense without resorting to WMD.

If, however, Iranian nuclear capability became imminent, the United States would have no choice but to provide post-Saddam Iraq with its own nuclear umbrella to counter any Iranian nuclear threats, assuming the relationship between the two countries was still hostile. The United States should also broker meetings between Iraqi and Israeli military leaders following Saddam's ouster, primarily in order to convince the former that Israel is not planning any attacks, nuclear or otherwise, against Iraq. Such meetings could be held secretly, perhaps in the United States, under the guise of officer training programs.

As for Iraq's intelligence services, all but three of the country's internal security apparatuses would need to be disbanded under a new regime, and all their personnel pensioned off. General Intelligence (al-Mukhabarat al-'Amma) is the most egregious human rights violator among these services, with a long history of torture, assassinations, executions, and other kinds of violent political repression. The three apparatuses that should be retained are the regular police, General Security (al-Amn al-'Amm), and the border police. Even these apparatuses would have to be purged of criminal and strongly pro-Saddam elements; nevertheless, they would be indispensable to a new regime.

In particular, the regular police would be needed to prevent crime—especially violent crime—from spiraling out of control after Saddam was toppled. As mentioned previously, once Iraq's corrupt internal security operatives were dismissed under a new regime, they would almost certainly attempt to form mafia-style crime syndicates in Iraq, similar to those established in Russia and Eastern Europe following the downfall of communist regimes. Therefore, the Iraqi regular police would need to be reinforced with reliable personnel. A post-Saddam regime should recruit highly educated individuals into the police investigative branches, especially those that specialize in anticorruption inquiries. Moreover, police salaries must be raised in order to minimize such corruption.

As for General Security, its ranks should be purged following Saddam's ouster and its remaining members then placed in charge of counterintelligence and counterinsurgency operations. Their methods should be changed as well: torture must be forbidden.

Finally, a post-Saddam regime would need to retain the border police, but only after purging corrupt officers involved in smuggling. Similarly, the military intelligence service should be effectively purged of all political elements and stripped of its authority in civilian areas.

Reconstituting the Educated Class

Given that Iraqis have been subjected to virulently xenophobic propaganda and terrible economic conditions for much of the past several decades, a new regime could be confronted with an Iraqi educated class that is hateful toward Jews and bitter toward the United States. Contrary to popular belief, this class has not disappeared from Iraq; rather, it was subsumed by Saddam's monstrous government expansion efforts during the 1970s. As a result, most well-educated Iraqis are now in government service.

Government salaries are insufficient to sustain a family, so the educated class has been in dire straits for quite some time. Most family property had to be sold to obtain food during the period before Saddam agreed to the United Nations (UN) oil-for-food program, and life in general has been in suspension for nearly a decade. Under such conditions, educated Iraqis have found it impossible to plan careers; instead, they must focus on day-to-day existence.

Until 1990, education was the main vehicle for upward mobility in Iraqi society. Since then, government job opportunities and wages have decreased dramatically, and many students have intentionally prolonged their studies in order to avoid conscription. Nevertheless, the educational system itself has not collapsed. For example, according to Iraqi government sources, the enrollment of new pupils at the primary, secondary, and university levels remained relatively stable between 1990 and 1996. Moreover, years of international sanctions have not had a significantly detrimental effect on the teacher-student ratio.[1] Improvements are needed in two key areas, however: teacher training and salary.

As for the Iraqi educated class in general, a new regime would need to invest great resources in retraining them not only in the art of government, but also in business management, new technologies, and various other areas of expertise that are needed in order to resuscitate the economy. Raising government salaries to reasonable levels would be insufficient; most government employees would have to be retrained with the goal of fulfilling their duties more effectively or leaving government service for the private sector.

A new regime would also need to reaffirm the status of higher education as a useful avenue toward developing a career and making a good living. Initially, government subsidies could be offered to help students study abroad, primarily in the West. Eventually, however, Iraqi universities should be restored to their pre-1990 eminence, particularly in the sciences, medicine, law, accountancy, Arabic, and English. Although a new regime would find intelligent and reasonably well-prepared cadres in all of these areas, the challenge would be to help them update their skills and choose careers that would benefit both themselves and their country.

Assimilating Returnees

Following the demise of Saddam's regime, many Iraqi expatriates would likely return to their country temporarily, in order to reunite with their families and assess the new situation. Patriotism notwithstanding, though, most of them would be unwilling to remain in post-Saddam Iraq, let alone invest in the economy, without solid evidence that the political system was stable and conducive to private enterprise. Attracting the massive reservoir of Iraqi talent from abroad should be a high priority for a new regime. For example, temporary tax exemptions could be offered to expatriates who were willing to invest foreign currency. Moreover, returning businesspeople and professionals would help to create jobs; for this reason alone, they would probably not be alienated by the rest of Iraqi society.

In addition to these expatriates, a new regime would likely have to assimilate a massive wave of up to 200,000 Shi'is returning from years of unhappy exile in Iran. Most of these Shi'is are very poor, and many are politically radical. Absorbing them would be a formidable task, but a post-Saddam regime should nevertheless make it a high priority, given the potentially destabilizing nature of such an influx.

Inevitably, certain returnees would have political ambitions, which could in turn spark competition and bitterness among rival factions. These ambitions could be forestalled temporarily by establishing a broad, interim governing coalition consisting of representatives from all significant Iraqi political groups. Yet, such a coalition would only be viable for a one- to two-year period following the fall of the current regime; eventually, democratic elections would need to be held. Given the emotionally charged atmosphere that would surely surround initial political campaigns and elections, the entire process would need to be placed under intense international scrutiny, with the international community emphasizing that Iraq would once again become a pariah state if the results of these elections were not respected.

Resuscitating the Economy

The Iraqi economy has begun to recover somewhat from the Gulf War and its aftermath, largely as a result of the oil-for-food program. With the glaring exception of the neglected Shi'i areas of southern Iraq, there is no shortage of food in the country. Although the food basket of most families is rather monotonous, and fresh food is still relatively expensive, the average daily intake of free food is more than 2,000 calories per capita. Similarly, hospitals outside the south are reasonably well stocked, aside from the more expensive medicines.

Nevertheless, the unemployment rate is currently thought to be around 25 percent, and it may in fact be much higher. The agricultural sector is still struggling due to shortages of fertilizer, spare parts, and machinery. Local industries, which are only beginning to revive, must cope with significant obstacles, including a severe power shortage. For example, the Baghdad area currently experiences power outages on a near daily basis, while provincial areas often go a third of each day without electricity.

Iraq's oil industry is unstable as well. Much damage was done to the Kirkuk oil fields during the post–Gulf War embargo years, when heavy fuel was pumped back into the ground without ascertaining its effects. Oil production has increased steadily since then, but in January 2000, a committee of experts sent to Iraq by the UN concluded that the production level of approximately 3 million barrels per day was unsustainable. This overproduction problem had arisen due to the Iraqis' use of deficient water-injection techniques and other high-risk solutions. Moreover, the industry is plagued by a shortage of spare parts, along with insufficient investment in operating costs, new oil wells and fields, and new technologies (e.g., horizontal drilling; three-dimensional seismic acquisition and reservoir simulation). Finally, oil storage facilities and transport systems related to the Turkish Kirkuk-Dortyol pipeline and the north-south Strategic Pipeline are in need of repairs, as are the Gulf terminals Mina al-Bakr and Khor al-Amaya.[2]

Before the invasion of Kuwait, the oil industry represented more than 90 percent of Iraq's export value. This trend would likely repeat itself in a post-Saddam, post-sanctions environment. Iraq's economic recovery would therefore depend on two basic components: a swift resuscitation of the oil industry combined with efforts toward debt consolidation and forgiveness. Hence, the most important contribution that Iraq's Gulf neighbors could make to a new regime would be debt forgiveness; at the very least, they should defer Iraq's debts for several years. Otherwise, they would risk fostering a weak and unstable neighbor, tottering indefinitely on the brink of economic and political collapse. Currently, the Gulf states' stance on this issue is unclear.

Near the end of the Iran-Iraq War, Saddam's regime promised the Iraqi public major postwar economic growth. These promises were unrealistic and resulted in a significant crisis of expectations; as the end of the 1980s approached, the Iraqi economy was not perceptibly resuscitated, unemployment was rampant, and the public was deeply disillusioned. In fact, these problems may have played a role in the regime's decision to invade Kuwait.

Today, the Iraqi public has similarly high expectations that the economy will take flight immediately after international sanctions are lifted. A new regime would have to dampen these expectations somewhat, even as it took decisive action to raise Iraqis' standard of living. For one thing, large-scale economic improvement takes time. Second, although the international community would be eager to lift sanctions as soon as possible following Saddam's ouster, it would first need assurances that the new regime was adamant about abandoning any pursuit of WMD.

Initially, then, a new regime would be best served by continuing the existing program of food rations, raising salaries to realistic levels, and decreasing unemployment by sponsoring professional development courses. For its part, the international community could further liberalize its import restrictions until it felt comfortable lifting them altogether. Moreover, the Iraqi people should be allowed to travel abroad freely, and restrictions on the media should be relaxed (with certain limitations on incitement left in place).

Securing Regional Cooperation

Despite his aggressive regional policies in the past, Saddam Husayn has managed to establish more or less stable relations with most of Iraq's neighbors—a mixture of economic cooperation, diplomatic exchanges, carefully calibrated border crossings, and mutual mistrust. Even Iraqi-Iranian relations are attaining a degree of normalcy; despite sporadic reminders that the war by proxy is not yet over, the two regimes have made significant economic and diplomatic overtures, and thousands of Iranian pilgrims travel to Iraq each month. Nevertheless, regime change could have a variety of ramifications on Iraq's relations with each of its neighbors, depending on the methods by which Saddam's regime is removed and the type of regime that replaces it.

Turkey

Turkey has not challenged Iraq's territorial status quo for several decades, aside from occasional, purely defensive military incursions into Iraqi Kurdish areas. Therefore, barring the prospect of Iraq splintering into smaller entities in the near future, Turkey will have little motivation to pursue Saddam's removal actively; its primary goal is a stable Iraq.

Ankara would be spurred to action, however, if it felt that Iraqi territorial integrity were threatened, particularly if the establishment of an independent Kurdish state or a Kurdish annexation of Kirkuk seemed imminent. In general, Turkey frowns on the prospect of a decentralized, federated Iraq, but Ankara's reaction to such a development would likely depend on the specific makeup of the resultant state.

Given the appropriate parameters, a federated Iraq would probably be the best option for both Iraqis and Turks. First, experience has shown that multiethnic states are more likely to remain stable if they adopt federal systems of governance. Second, a federal arrangement would be the best way of ensuring equitable resource distribution and political representation for minorities. For example, such a system could reassure the Kurds that they would not be subjected to economic or political discrimination, even if they had to abandon their claims on Kirkuk. In fact, Saddam himself was willing to give the Kurds central representation, as he showed in his March 1970 agreement with Mulla Mustafa al-Barzani. Third, a federated Iraq, if structured appropriately, could meet all of Turkey's principal criteria for an ideal neighbor: a stable country that is willing and able to guard the border against Kurdish militant infiltration, to buy large quantities of Turkish products, and to send as much oil as possible through the twin pipelines from Kirkuk to Dortyol.

The United States will need to secure Turkey's goodwill in order to topple Saddam. At the same time, however, it will need to appease the Iraqi Kurds. A federated Iraq is perhaps the best means of mediating between these conflicting interests.

Iran

Iran is content with a relatively isolated and contained Saddam holding the reins of power in Iraq, particularly when the likely alternative is a pro-American regime in Baghdad. Moreover, the Iranian old guard, led by Ayatollah 'Ali Khamene'i and the security establishment, feel that a democratic regime in Iraq would provide the liberals in Tehran with a dangerous example. Nevertheless, Iran would be highly unlikely to invade a newly democratic Iraq, given the certainty of a devastating American reaction.

Iran could resort to other means of destabilizing a new Iraqi regime, however, including sedition, terrorist activity, and guerrilla warfare. For example, Tehran could sponsor terrorist operations by Shi'i fundamentalists in southern Iraq and in Baghdad itself (nearly 70 percent of the capital's population is Shi'i), perhaps even fostering a breakaway Shi'i buffer province in the south. Iran would likely sponsor terrorist activity against U.S. troops as well. Such violence could erupt even if the vast majority of Iraqi Shi'is are supportive of both the new regime and the American military presence. In this case, the United States would have little choice but to retaliate emphatically against Iran; only a heavy price would force Tehran to rethink its policy.

The best way to counter Iran's destabilizing efforts would be through the rehabilitation of the Iraqi infrastructure and economy and the provision of adequate political representation to the Iraqi public. A post-Saddam regime would need to demonstrate that it could offer the Iraqi people—particularly those in the south and the border areas—much more than Tehran could. Given the Arab identity of much of the Iraqi population, a new regime would have no problem achieving this goal, as long as it put its priorities in the proper order.

Other Neighbors

If Saddam were removed, Syria would do everything in its power to control the new regime in Baghdad, primarily through its own supporters among the Iraqi opposition. Such a takeover must be prevented. A new Iraqi regime could use the prospect of accelerated economic exchange as a means of moderating Syrian political infiltration, emphasizing Syria's dependence on Iraqi buying power and oil exports through the Haditha-Banias pipeline. In any case, a post-Saddam regime should be ready to pay an economic price in order to maintain peace and sovereignty.

Jordan depends on Iraqi trade more than any other neighbor. Currently, Jordan imports 50 percent of its oil from Iraq free of charge, and most of Jordan's industries are geared toward the Iraqi market. Therefore, a new Iraqi regime would find Jordan a willing partner in economic cooperation. For example, Amman would welcome the construction of an Iraqi oil pipeline through Jordan to the Red Sea once Iraqi oil production reached the appropriate levels.

Kuwait would have an obvious interest in a new, more peaceful Iraqi regime. Almost any new regime would be acceptable, provided it were not built around Saddam's children or the Ba'ath old guard. As described previously, though, Kuwait should be prepared to forgive Iraqi debts in order to help stabilize a new regime.

Finally, if Saddam's regime were toppled, Saudi Arabia would likely prefer that another totalitarian regime replace it, as long as this regime continued the current rapprochement between the two countries (which it most likely would). The Saudis would take issue with a democratic Iraqi regime, but not to the extent that they would risk a political confrontation with the United States. Yet, they could attempt to destabilize such a regime by insisting on complete debt repayment.

Conclusion

Despite all of the potential obstacles to regime change and reform, Iraqi society holds great promise. Iraqis have experienced the most horrendous Arab dictatorship in the modern age, so they are likely to appreciate freedom once it is in sight. The liberal opposition in particular would be amenable to reform; although they cannot topple Saddam on their own, they could play a crucial role in guiding the democratization process. Moreover, Iraqi society as a whole is better educated than most other Arab societies, particularly in the sciences. These and other factors represent a solid base on which a new regime could build. When supported by a superpower like the United States, such a regime would stand a good chance of success.

These prospects would be enhanced if the new regime were fully aware of the pitfalls that it might encounter as it assumed full control of the country. Post-Saddam Iraq could well become the first Arab democracy, but this process would have to be gradual and could require significant Western sponsorship. Moreover, a new regime would have to convince the Iraqi people that the petrified national economy would soon revive, that they would be able to plan their lives again, and that political activity would be permitted, even if within clear limits. This is a tall order, but given Iraq's vast material and human resources, it is not unrealistic.

Notes

1. See Maha A. Eskandar, "Trends of Education Growth in Iraq during the Period 1968/9–1996/7," in *Population and Sustainable Development*, Population and Development Research Monograph Series No. 6 (Cairo: Cairo Demographic Center, 1999), pp. 531–546.

2. Information on the Iraqi oil industry was compiled from the following sources: U.S. Energy Information Administration, *Iraq* (Washington, D.C.: U.S. Government Printing Office, September 2000), pp. 2–6; United Nations Security Council, *Report of the Secretary General Pursuant to Paragraphs 28 and 30 of Resolution 1284 (1999) and Paragraph 5 of Resolution 1281* (March 10, 2000), pp. 3–11; United Nations, *Report of the Secretary General Pursuant to Paragraph 5 of Security Council Resolution 1281 (1999)* (June 1, 2000), chapters IIa, IIIb.